T0311446

Cambridge Elements ≡

Elements in Philosophy of Mind
edited by
Keith Frankish
The University of Sheffield

HUMAN REASONING

David E. Over
University of Durham
Jonathan St B. T. Evans
University of Plymouth

CAMBRIDGE
UNIVERSITY PRESS

CAMBRIDGE
UNIVERSITY PRESS

Shaftesbury Road, Cambridge CB2 8EA, United Kingdom

One Liberty Plaza, 20th Floor, New York, NY 10006, USA

477 Williamstown Road, Port Melbourne, VIC 3207, Australia

314–321, 3rd Floor, Plot 3, Splendor Forum, Jasola District Centre,
New Delhi – 110025, India

103 Penang Road, #05–06/07, Visioncrest Commercial, Singapore 238467

Cambridge University Press is part of Cambridge University Press & Assessment,
a department of the University of Cambridge.

We share the University's mission to contribute to society through the pursuit of
education, learning and research at the highest international levels of excellence.

www.cambridge.org
Information on this title: www.cambridge.org/9781009495363

DOI: 10.1017/9781009495349

When citing this work, please include a reference to the DOI 10.1017/9781009495349

First published 2024

A catalogue record for this publication is available from the British Library.

ISBN 978-1-009-49536-3 Hardback
ISBN 978-1-009-49531-8 Paperback
ISSN 2633-9080 (online)
ISSN 2633-9072 (print)

Human Reasoning

Elements in Philosophy of Mind

DOI: 10.1017/9781009495349
First published online: May 2024

David E. Over
University of Durham

Jonathan St B. T. Evans
University of Plymouth

Author for correspondence: David E. Over, david.over@durham.ac.uk

Abstract: This Element is on new developments in the psychology of reasoning that raise or address philosophical questions. In traditional studies in the psychology of reasoning, the focus was on inference from arbitrary assumptions and not at all from beliefs, and classical binary logic was presupposed as the only standard for human reasoning. But recently a new Bayesian paradigm has emerged in the discipline. This views ordinary human reasoning as mostly inferring probabilistic conclusions from degrees of beliefs, or from hypothetical premises relevant to a purpose at hand, and as often about revising or updating degrees of belief. This Element also covers new formulations of dual-process theories of the mind, stating that there are two types of mental processing, one rapid and intuitive and shared with other animals, and the other slow and reflective and more characteristic of human beings. Finally, we discuss implications for human rationality.

Keywords: new paradigm, dual processes, Bayesian reasoning, probability judgement, human rationality.

ISBNs: 9781009495363 (HB), 9781009495318 (PB), 9781009495349 (OC)
ISSNs: 2633-9080 (online), 2633-9072 (print)

Contents

1 Introduction

Reasoning is the inferring of conclusions from premises, and this Element is an account of what psychologists have discovered about human reasoning. We have not found it hard to select topics for it. Two broad contemporary themes in the psychology of reasoning have been influenced by logicians and philosophers and clearly raise philosophical questions.

The first of these themes is the emergence of a *new paradigm* in the psychology of reasoning, replacing with Bayesian subjective probability theory the traditional presupposition that classical logic and its conditional set the normative standard for human reasoning. This theme is primarily found in Sections 2–5. Section 5 has at its core the psychological findings on the hypothesis that the probability of the natural language conditional, *P(if p then q)*, is the conditional probability of *q* given *p*, *P(q|p)*. This hypothesis was first stated by philosophical logicians and has long been of great interest to them, and its confirmation in psychological experiments, for many conditionals, in turn supports the new Bayesian paradigm. More generally, logicians and philosophers, going back at least to de Finetti and Ramsey, have substantially influenced the new paradigm, as will become clear in our references.

The second theme is research in psychology on *dual-process* theories of the mind. These state that there are two types of mental processes, one rapid and intuitive and shared with other animals, and the other slow and reflective and more characteristic of human beings. Section 6 is on this topic, explaining how the psychological understanding of it has been deepened and refined over time. Philosophers have helped in this process, and no doubt will continue to do so. Here, as elsewhere, we cite relevant philosophical as well as psychological work.

Section 7 concerns what the new paradigm and new forms of dual-process theory tell us about human rationality, epistemic and instrumental. This section rapidly leads to normative and philosophical questions that have to be left in philosophical hands.

The psychology of reasoning, as we define it, is the science in which hypotheses and theories about human reasoning are proposed and tested in experiments. Human participants are asked to solve reasoning problems under controlled conditions, with features of the problems manipulated to address theoretical questions (Evans, 2005). Most of these experiments have had literate participants, but there have also been studies of participants who do not have or use a written language (Boissin et al., 2024). The answers people give, and sometimes the speed with which they do so, inform us about the nature of the mental processes they use. This field has always paid attention to the writing of philosophers about how they believe people should reason. The results have informed both philosophy and psychology alike. In this Element, we summarise the essential psychological findings and their implications for philosophers.

2 Deductive Reasoning

The importance of *classical logic* (Shapiro & Kissel, 2022) is widely recognised. It is binary in having truth and falsity as its only truth values, and the conclusions of its *valid* inferences are true assuming that the premises are true. Psychologists working on human thinking and reasoning in the mid twentieth century presupposed that classical validity was the only logical standard for human rationality, and this had a profound influence on the psychology of reasoning. It led to hundreds of published experiments using the *deduction paradigm* (Evans, 2002) based on classical logic. To contrast it with later developments, we will sometimes call this the *traditional* approach or paradigm. This field of work was directly or indirectly inspired by philosophical writing, and it is of importance that philosophers be aware of the findings that were reported. A detailed review of this period of work is in Evans et al. (1993) and a brief summary follows in this section. This traditional approach dominated the field until around 1990, when a number of authors started to call for a different approach, now known as the 'new paradigm psychology of reasoning' (Oaksford & Chater, 2020; Over, 2009, 2020). This new approach made degrees of belief and so subjective probability judgements central to the study of human reasoning. The relevant normative standards for it are *probability theory* and *probability logic* (Demey et al., 2023).

2.1 The Deduction Paradigm

One huge influence on the psychology of reasoning was the work of the Swiss psychologist Jean Piaget who argued that children's thinking develops through a series of stages which conclude with that of formal operational thought. This meant that adults were supposed to be able to reason abstractly and hypothetically (Inhelder & Piaget, 1958). Error and bias had been reported in very early psychological studies of reasoning (Wilkins, 1928; Woodworth & Sells, 1935), but some psychologists argued that these studies were misleading. People's underlying reasoning could be logical but obscured by a failure to apply reasoning to the problem set, or by misinterpreting the given information, so that they were in effect reasoning from different premises than those assumed by the experimenter (Henle, 1962; Smedslund, 1970). However, the idea that human reasoning was basically logical was also subjected to strong empirical challenge, for example in the early studies of the British psychologist Peter Wason and his colleagues (Wason & Johnson-Laird, 1972).

In the traditional paradigm, experimenters asked people to evaluate or generate logical arguments, with their answers compared with classical logical norms to assess their correctness. Psychologists took the view that people ought to be innately logical and that they should therefore not have had formal logical instruction. Indeed, it is standard practice with this method to exclude people who have received any formal training in logic. In more detail, the method consisted of asking participants in an experiment to *assume* the truth of given premises, which were sometimes abstract, arbitrary, or unbelievable. They were then asked whether a given conclusion necessarily followed, or to infer a conclusion which necessarily followed. The term 'necessarily' in these instructions was rarely defined for the participants (but see Lassiter & Goodman, 2015, on how they might understand it).

The other key component in the deduction paradigm was the use of classical logic as the normative theory for deciding whether the deductions made are correct or incorrect. This is noteworthy because outside of the study of reasoning and decision-making, normative theory is rarely used in cognitive psychology. Only in the study of reasoning and decision-making do psychologists and philosophers debate rationality. For example, no one is described as irrational for failing to remember a long list of words or being unable to read tiny print, but people have been accused of irrationality for reasoning illogically, or for violating the axioms of decision theory. It is also striking that the majority (but by no means all) of the psychologists working on reasoning have had until recently only an elementary understanding of logic, confined mostly to classical logic. The problem of alternative normative accounts (see Section 7) was not addressed by psychologists until most of the deduction studies had been published (but see Elqayam & Evans, 2011, Oaksford & Chater, 2007, and Stanovich, 1999). The great bulk of studies in the deduction paradigm have used Aristotelian syllogisms or conditional inferences, and we will briefly summarise this work and its main findings in Sections 2.2–2.6.

2.2 Classical Syllogisms

Psychologists have extensively used the syllogisms first described by Aristotle (Kneale & Kneale, 1962) to study deductive reasoning. Each syllogism consists of two assumed premises and an inferred conclusion. The three terms related in a syllogism are often described as *S* and *P*, representing the subject and predicate of the conclusions, and *M*, a middle term which links them, as in

Some M are P, All S are M
Therefore, Some S are P

A realistic version of the above might be

> Some scientists are astronomers
> All psychologists are scientists
> Therefore, Some psychologists are astronomers

This argument is clearly invalid. It is possible that some psychologists are also astronomers but there is no necessary reason why they should be, given the premises. However, participants are much more likely to say this argument is valid than invalid when it is given in an abstract form, such as Some A are B, All C are A, therefore Some C are B.

The premises and conclusions may each take one of four different forms, classically known as A (*All A are B*), E (*No A are B*), I (*Some A are B*) and O (*Some A are not B*). The *mood* of the syllogisms is determined by these forms. For example, the above argument has the mood IAI. Syllogisms can also have *figures*, depending on how the terms are arranged. The above syllogism is in figure one: M-P, S-M, S-P. Assuming that the conclusion is always of the form S-P, there are three other ways to arrange the terms, for example, P-M, S-M, S-P is in figure two. With 64 possible moods and four possible figures, there are 256 distinct syllogisms. Of these a mere 24 are valid in Aristotelian logic, even allowing weak conclusions, such as *Some S are P* when *All S are P* could have been concluded. *Some S are P* does not validly follow from *All S are P* in contemporary classical logic (Shapiro & Kissel, 2022), which implies that *All S are P* is true when *S* is an empty term. But this difference will not affect our psychological points here. From a psychological point of view, we can double the number of syllogisms by switching the positions of the first and second premises. Though this does not affect the logic, it can and does affect the inferences ordinary people draw.

The psychological studies divide into those using abstract terms (typically the letters *A*, *B* and *C*) and those using realistic content. Both have provided interesting findings, and we consider the abstract reasoning first. The standout finding of the abstract studies is that people endorse the conclusions of most syllogisms, even though the great bulk of them are invalid. To our knowledge, only one published study (Evans et al., 1999) presented every possible combination of moods and figures, with participants asked in one group to judge whether the conclusion was *necessary* (equivalent to valid), and in another whether it was *possible*, given the premises. (The authors provided an appendix showing the percentage saying 'Yes' in each case.) Asked to judge the necessity (validity) of conclusions given the premises, participants accepted about 72 per cent that were valid conclusions, around 45 per cent that were invalid but possible conclusions, but only 10 per cent that were logically impossible given the premises. So clearly there was some understanding of the logic being shown, but with very high error rates. When asked if the same conclusions were possible, these numbers increased in all cases, so that 'possible' seemed to participants simply to be a cautious form of 'necessary'. The effect was greatest for syllogisms with possible conclusions, but still present for necessary and impossible ones. Basically, and contrary to both logic and the instructions, participants like to endorse conclusions unless there is a clear reason not to do so. The overwhelming finding in this research is the very high endorsement rate of fallacies. Abstract syllogistic reasoning is clearly very difficult for (typically) university student participants when not trained in logic.

Both the mood and the figure of the syllogisms also bias the judgement of validity. It was claimed in the earliest study (Woodworth & Sells, 1935) that people like to endorse conclusions which match the mood of the premises, the so-called *atmosphere effect*. While this finding has been broadly replicated in later studies (Evans et al., 1993), more nuanced psychological accounts of the precise nature of the bias have been developed (e.g., Chater & Oaksford, 1999). The figure of the syllogisms also biases reasoning, in that people generally prefer conclusions in which the order of the terms corresponds with their order of presentation in the premises. This has been observed both when people generate their own conclusions (Johnson-Laird & Bara, 1984) and when conclusions are given for evaluation (Morley et al., 2004). In brief, abstract syllogistic reasoning is very difficult for ordinary people, who make many logical mistakes, frequently endorse fallacious conclusions as necessary and are systematically biased by logically irrelevant variants of the presentation (see Oaksford & Chater, 2020, for new paradigm studies of syllogisms).

2.3 The Belief Bias Effect

One of the most important findings in the study of syllogistic reasoning arises when realistic content is introduced. As Wilkins (1928) observed almost a century ago, people's judgements of validity are influenced by whether or not they believe the conclusion. After a number of early reports based on questionable methodology, the basic phenomena of *belief bias* were established by Evans et al. (1983) followed by a flurry of research interest which persists to the current day in the psychology of reasoning (see Evans et al., 2022, for a recent review). Evans et al. (1983) devised syllogisms which fitted into four categories, depending on the validity of the arguments and the believability of the conclusions. Hence, conclusions could be Valid-Believable (VB), Valid-Unbelievable (VU), Invalid-Believable (IB), and Invalid-Unbelievable (IU). Comparing performance on these four types lead to three clear findings, all highly statistically significant, which have been replicated many times since:

1. Validity effect. People endorse more valid than invalid arguments, that is (VB+VU) > (IU+IB)
2. Belief effect. People endorse more arguments with believable than unbelievable conclusions, that is (VB+IB) > (VU+IU)
3. Interaction effect. Belief bias is larger for invalid arguments, that is (IB-IU) > (VB-VU).

All three effects are about equally large and highly reliable. Figure 1 shows the endorsement rates of the combined experiments of Evans et al., 1983. Most replication studies show a statistically significant belief bias for valid as well as invalid arguments, but of smaller size, as Figure 1 clearly illustrates.

To illustrate the findings with some examples, the participants in the Evans et al. (1983) study found the following argument quite compelling, with 71 per cent declaring it valid:

> No addictive things are inexpensive
> Some cigarettes are inexpensive
> Therefore, some addictive things are not cigarettes

By contrast they were very unimpressed with this argument; only 10 per cent thought it valid:

> No millionaires are hard workers
> Some rich people are hard workers
> Therefore, some millionaires are not rich people

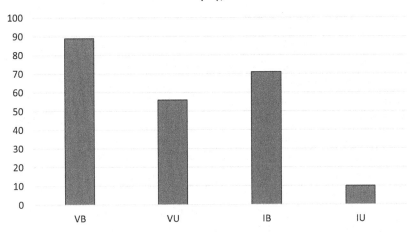

Endorsment rates (%), Evans et al. 1983

Figure 1 Percentage of conclusions endorsed as valid in the study of Evans et al. (1983) for valid-believable (VB), valid-unbelievable (VU), invalid-believable (IB), invalid-unbelievable (IU) syllogisms

The two arguments have precisely the same logical form and neither is valid. The difference is that people believe the first conclusion and disbelieve the second.

However, the belief bias effect in syllogistic reasoning (demonstrated with other reasoning tasks) does *not* mean that participants ignore the logic, when clearly instructed to assess the necessity of the conclusion given the premises. Rather it suggests that there is some kind of conflict between the logical task and influence of belief. Evans et al. (1983) showed that this was not due, as one might suppose, to some participants using logic and others belief, but rather that the conflict was within individual reasoners. That is, people would sometimes go with logic but other times with belief. This was one of the key findings that lent support to dual-process theories of reasoning discussed in Section 6. The interaction of belief with validity may relate to the general finding that people are all too willing to endorse fallacies generally. One reason to withhold an inference might be perception of its invalidity, but another could be the unbelievability of its conclusion. Various authors have suggested that people might be more motivated to disapprove of an argument and look for a counterexample case when they disbelieve its conclusion (Evans, 2007a).

De Neys (2012) surprisingly found that belief–logic conflict may be detected rapidly and preconsciously, reflected in response times, confidence levels and autonomic responses, leading to an argument that there may be 'logical intuitions' (but see Section 6.3). Moreover, the logic of the problem can interfere when people are instructed to respond on the basis of belief (Handley et al., 2011). These findings seem very odd. How could one know whether an argument was valid or not, without first engaging in a slow process of reasoning? However, such studies have generally used very much simpler logical arguments than classical syllogisms (Section 6.3), which may not engage working memory (Evans, 2019). What all these studies demonstrate beyond doubt, however, is that most people find it difficult or impossible to disregard their prior beliefs *completely* when engaged in a deductive reasoning task.

Traditional studies of syllogistic reasoning did point the way to the new paradigm by showing clearly that this reasoning could not be fully explained without taking account of people's beliefs. Sections 3–5 will be on the new paradigm topics of how belief should influence reasoning and how it actually does.

2.4 Conditional Syllogisms

Another major paradigm in the psychology of deductive reasoning, the *conditional inference task*, presented its participants with conditional syllogisms for evaluation, again with two assumed premises and an inferred conclusion. As with classical syllogisms, these problems can be given with abstract or thematic content. They are somewhat simpler, however, since they relate only two rather than three terms. Participants are usually tasked with the following four argument types to evaluate:

Modus Ponens (MP)
If the letter is A then the number is 4; the letter is A, therefore the number is 4.
Denial of the Antecedent (DA)
If the letter is A then the number is 4; the letter is not-A, therefore the number is not-4.
Affirmation of the Consequent (AC)
If the letter is A then the number is 4; the number is 4, therefore the letter is A.
Modus Tollens (MT)
If the letter is A then the number is 4; the number is not-4, therefore the letter is not-A.

Of these inferences, MP and MT are valid, and DA and AC are invalid, in both classical logic and probability logic (Evans & Over, 2004). While frequencies of endorsement vary somewhat between different studies in the literature, there are some very clear trends when materials are abstract, as in the above examples. MP is endorsed very highly, with a number of studies reporting 100 per cent acceptance rates. MT, the other valid inference, is endorsed far less frequently, about 60 per cent of the time. The two fallacies, AC and DA, are frequently endorsed but the extent varies considerably across studies. The latter finding could be accounted for by assuming that people adopt a biconditional interpretation or accept invited pragmatic inferences (Evans & Over, 2004). This cannot explain the difficulty with MT inferences, which is valid on all plausible pragmatic interpretations, but see Section 3.4 on these inferences.

Generally speaking, individual differences in general intelligence correlate highly with finding the normatively correct solution to reasoning and decision problems (Stanovich, 2011). In line with this, there is evidence that participants of higher general intelligence are better able to suppress the fallacies AC and DA in abstract conditional inference (Evans, Handley et al., 2007; Newstead et al., 2004). However, the same studies show, surprisingly, that high-ability participants draw *fewer* valid MT inferences. One possible explanation is that MT is hard for people to draw when a genuine attempt at deductive reasoning is being made (but again see Section 3.4 on MT). Lower-ability participants might also engage in simple equivalence reasoning. Given *if p then q*, they may expect *p* and *q* to go together, although this cannot explain the full pattern of findings (Evans et al., 2007).

The difficulty of MT became a focus for an argument between theorists favouring a *mental models* account of deductive reasoning (Johnson-Laird, 1983; Johnson-Laird & Byrne, 1991) and those offering a *mental logic* account

(Braine & O'Brien, 1991; Rips, 1994). Mental logic theorists argued that people use an innate 'natural logic' comprised of *natural deduction* inference rules, some of which take a simple, direct form. An example of such a rule is *and-elimination*, inferring *p* from *p & q* (see also Section 3.2). Such inferences are said to be made automatically and without effort, drawing on implicit rules that are effectively part of the language processing system. Other inferences can only be made by high effort, and presumably conscious, indirect reasoning strategies. For example, as in classical natural deduction theories proposed by logicians (Shapiro & Kissel, 2022), there is no direct rule for MT in mental logic. It can only be derived indirectly using *reductio ad absurdum* reasoning. In the above example, one would suppose that there was an A, and if there were an A then there would be a 4. Since there is not a 4, the supposition of that there is an A must be false by a reductio. However, this indirect reasoning is hypothesised to be slow and error prone compared with the direct MP. The latter follows immediately from an inference rule built into the natural language meaning of *if* in the mental logic account.

Mental model theory, by contrast, denies that there are any inference rules in the head, and proposes instead that deduction is based on a simple semantic principle: an inference is valid if there is no counterexample to it. In this account, people construct and use mental models in reasoning to represent possible states of the world and search for counterexample models to try to infer or test the validity of inferences. Presumably this is at least in part a conscious process because core to the theory and its predictions is the claim that mental models load working memory, increasingly so when they are more complex or more than one needs to be considered. MP is simple and immediate because the *p & q* case is the default mental model that is used to represent *if p then q*, along with initially unspecified other possibilities. When presented with the premise *not-q*, no inference will follow unless the individual tries to 'flesh out' other states of the world (models) that could be consistent with the conditional statement. These additional models are: *not-p & q* and *not p & not q*, with only *p & not-q* being excluded. On this basis, only the second of these models is consistent with a conditional statement in which *not-q* also holds, and it yields the *not-p* conclusion. But again, this reasoning process is supposed to be indirect, difficult, and prone to error (see Section 3.1 for more on the conditional in mental model theory).

Conditional inferences have also been studied with a variety of realistic content, which can affect the rates with which the conclusions are inferred in the four inferences (Byrne, 1989; Stevenson & Over, 1995). Of particular importance are the real-world beliefs that participants hold about the relationship between *p* and *q*, for a conditional statement *if p then q*. Studies have manipulated whether the occurrence of *p* appears to be either a sufficient or necessary condition for q with particular contents. It is not perceived as necessary when people can easily think of alternative antecedents which would lead to q, and it is not perceived as sufficient when they can think of disabling conditions which would prevent p leading to q. The basic finding is that the valid inferences MP and MT, are suppressed when perceived sufficiency is low, implying that $P(q|p)$ is low, and the fallacies, AC and DA, are suppressed when perceived necessity is low, implying $P(p|q)$ is low. Classical logic only guarantees that MP and MT lead to true conclusions from true premises. If the premises are in some doubt, say because of low sufficiency, the conclusion can rightly be doubted as well. However, the suppression findings are retained when the participants are told to assume that the premises are true (Thompson, 1994). Under these instructions, some participants violate classical logic. They may find it hard to assume what they do not believe, and finding the premises uncertain, they may take the conclusion to be uncertain as well (see Sections 3.2 and 5.2). It could therefore be argued that confidence in the conclusion is what is sometimes 'suppressed' and not the inference itself (Over & Cruz, 2018).

A later study demonstrated belief bias more directly in conditional reasoning by showing that all four inferences, both valid and invalid, could be suppressed when participants had low belief in the conditional statement (Evans et al., 2010). This effect, however, depended both upon the instructions given and the cognitive ability of the participants. One group were given *deductive reasoning instructions*, being told to assume the premises were true and asked to decide if the conclusion necessarily followed. Another group were given *pragmatic reasoning instructions* that made no reference to assuming the premises and were asked to judge their degree of belief in the conclusion. All participants were given a test of general intelligence and split into subgroups high and low on this measure. Under pragmatic reasoning instructions, participants of all abilities showed a similar belief effect, in that they assigned lower ratings to conclusions drawn from unbelievable conditional statements. Under deductive reasoning instructions, however, the belief bias effect was restricted to lower-ability participants only. This finding is important as few studies of deductive reasoning have included intelligence measures. It indicates that people of higher cognitive ability are better able to comply with instructions to assume the truth of the premises. Participants of lower cognitive ability are less able to do this and tend to display belief bias.

In a new paradigm approach (Section 2.6), we would ask how far being less able to follow instructions to assume premises is a serious bias that limits rationality (Section 7). But these findings are consistent with the broader individual differences research programme of Keith Stanovich, who argues that higher intelligence facilitates the ability to 'decouple' beliefs and reason hypothetically (Stanovich, 2011). We will discuss his programme of work in detail in Section 6.

2.5 Summary of Findings with the Deduction Paradigm

Had space permitted, we might also have discussed here the extensive research carried out with the Wason selection task (Wason, 1966). The selection task has traditionally been seen as a deductive reasoning problem and studied by the same researchers as well as others not normally working in the psychology of reasoning. This has produced a rich set of findings (see Evans, 2022, for a recent review). The task itself will be covered in Section 6.1, but suffice it to say for now that work on the selection task supports the same general conclusions which we can draw from the deduction studies briefly reviewed in this section. These are as follows:

1. Untrained participants show some degree of deductive competence: their responses are generally influenced, at least in part, by the logical validity of the arguments presented to them.
2. There is a strong general tendency to endorse invalid arguments whose conclusions could be true but are not necessitated by the premises.
3. Participants are subject to a number of cognitive biases in reasoning, making systematic as well as random errors.
4. When realistic content is used, people are almost always influenced by their prior knowledge and belief about the content and context.
5. People higher in general intelligence generally are better able to reason logically and ignore prior belief, but only if they are given strict deductive reasoning instructions.

Taken as a whole, the above findings suggest that either much real-world reasoning is irrational, or else that the yardstick for rationality should not simply be classically valid inferences from assumptions. Of course, being unable to suspend one's beliefs when instructed to do so by a psychologist in an experiment cannot, in itself, be irrational. As a result, this experimental work, along with that in other fields of reasoning and decision-making, has initiated a great rationality debate (see Evans, 2021, and Section 7). Dissatisfaction with the traditional approach and its associated deductive paradigm has also led to the new paradigm in the psychology of reasoning, which we continue to describe in the next and later sections.

2.6 New Paradigm Psychology of Reasoning

What is often referred to as the 'new paradigm' is not very precisely defined other than negatively. It is the psychological study of human reasoning that has moved away from the definition of normativity based on classical binary logic, in which all propositions are assumed to be true or false, with no account taken of their subjective probabilities. The original use of 'new paradigm psychology of reasoning' was to refer to studies that placed subjective probability judgements at the centre of the field (Over, 2009). But for some psychologists, the problem is not just a demand to reason from assumptions in classical logic, but the use of a strong normative theory to assess human reasoning, obscuring the psychological study. It has been argued that the psychology of reasoning should fall in line with the rest of cognitive psychology by focussing on *what* people do, rather than recording errors and biases (Elqayam & Evans, 2011; Evans, 2002). This change encourages a much deeper focus on pragmatics in reasoning (Bonnefon, 2013).

However, there is also a strong tradition and contemporary practice of proposing alternative normative models to classical logic for reasoning (Over, 2020). A sustained research programme of this type has been run by the psychologists Mike Oaksford and Nick Chater, dating from their seminal paper on the Wason selection task, in which they argued that the standard 'erroneous' responses could have a rational explanation from a different viewpoint (Oaksford & Chater, 1994). Oaksford and Chater (2007) argued influentially that Bayesian subjective probability theory could replace classical logic as the norm for human reasoning. Philosophers contributed to the paradigm shift. L. Jonathan Cohen's (1981) critique of the psychology of reasoning and decision-making, which will be covered in Section 7, directly challenged psychologists' use of standard normative theories. Also very influential was Edgington (1995) on the natural language conditional *if p then q* (the first author learned much from having her as his PhD supervisor). She explained the problems of claiming that *if p then q* is logically equivalent to the classical *material conditional*, itself logically equivalent to *not-p or q*. This claim was implicitly assumed to be correct in much psychological work at that time (but see Braine & O'Brien, 1991, and Rips, 1994, for dissenting voices).

Edgington (1995) argued strongly (see originally Adams, 1965) for what we will call *the Equation* and, in experimental contexts, *the conditional probability hypothesis*. The Equation/conditional probability hypothesis states that the subjective probability of the natural language conditional *P(if p then q)* is the conditional subjective probability of *q* given *p*:

$$P(if\ p\ then\ q) = P(q|p)$$

In the early twenty-first century, psychologists demonstrated that ordinary people generally conform to this hypothesis. For the first experimental studies of it, see Evans et al. (2003), Oberauer and Wilhelm (2003), and Over et al. (2007). Section 5 covers later studies.

A book published by the current authors (Evans & Over, 2004) drew together philosophical and psychological work on conditionals and proposed a *suppositional* theory of conditionals (see Section 5.1), linked to broader theory of *hypothetical thinking*, in which $P(if\ p\ then\ q) = P(q|p)$. Following this work, a major field of study of conditionals within the new paradigm has developed, with a range of logical ideas being taken from philosophy and applied in a psychological context (see Sections 3, 5, and 6). The traditional deduction paradigm has not been entirely abandoned, however. For example, it is still relevant to the study of dual processes in reasoning (Section 6), as it requires what is known as Type 2 processing – high effort, loading on working memory – to comply with the instructions to assume the premises of inferences, disregarding belief, and find conclusions that necessarily follow. Only some people with special training, or relatively high cognitive ability, are able follow such instructions fully and reliably.

3 Reasoning and Probability

The psychology of reasoning started out presupposing that 'correct' reasoning is simply classically valid inference from premises assumed to be true. In contrast, the new paradigm, as we interpret it, stresses that most reasoning, in science and everyday affairs, takes place in a context of uncertainty. It is from premises which are beliefs or hypotheses with reasonable probabilities, or it is about possible actions in decision-making (Over, 2020). The difference between the traditional paradigm and the new paradigm is particularly marked in theories of the natural language conditional. In this section, we will explain why the new paradigm rejected the traditional presupposition that the natural language conditional is equivalent to the classical material conditional, and also cover the logical and philosophical foundations of the new paradigm.

3.1 The Material Conditional in Psychology

The mental model theory of Johnson-Laird and Byrne (1991) is the best example of the claim in traditional psychology of reasoning that a fully modelled, or analysed, natural language conditional, *if p then q*, is equivalent to the material conditional of classical logic, which is, in turn, logically equivalent to *not-p or q*. One of their examples was:

(3.1) If Arthur is in Edinburgh (*d*), then Carol is in Glasgow (*g*).

Johnson-Laird and Byrne held that (3.1) is true when Arthur is in Edinburgh, and Carol is in Glasgow, and false when Arthur is in Edinburgh, and Carol is not in Glasgow. They then asked, 'But, suppose its antecedent is false, i.e. Arthur is *not* in Edinburgh, is the conditional true or false?', and answered, 'It can hardly be false, and so since the propositional calculus allows only truth or falsity, it must be true' (Johnson-Laird and Byrne, 1991, p. 7). The propositional calculus is the branch of classical logic for reasoning with the connectives *not*, *and*, and *or*, and so Johnson-Laird and Byrne were clearly presupposing here, without argument, that the correct logic for the natural language conditional (3.1) is bivalent and truth functional. They agreed with many other theorists that (3.1) is true when *d* is true and *g* is true, and false when *d* is true and *g* is false. But then Johnson-Laird and Byrne appealed to classical logic to infer that (3.1) is true when *d* is false and *g* is true, and true when *d* is false and *g* is false. They are presupposing that (3.1) is logically equivalent to *not-d or g*. This *material conditional analysis* of the natural language conditional is summarised in Table 1.

Johnson-Laird and Byrne (1991, pp. 73–74) accepted the *paradoxes* of the material conditional analysis. The first paradox is that this analysis implies the logical validity of inferring *if p then q* from *not-p*, and the second paradox is that it implies the logical validity of inferring *if p then q* from *q*. They rightly wrote that we must decide ' . . . to abandon this analysis of the conditional . . ., or to accept the validity of these apparently paradoxical inferences and to explain why they seem improper', and they added, 'We shall embrace the second alternative'. They went on to argue that these inferences appear paradoxical because they 'throw semantic informative away'. In other words, the conclusion is less informative than the premise.

It is true that in cooperative communication we would not, generally, want to deny our hearers information by making an assertion that we had inferred from one with more semantic information (compare Grice, 1989, on these paradoxes). But we do not have to worry about communicating well with other people when we are making inferences from our own degrees of belief, for our own benefit. For example, suppose we are wondering whether to invest in a cryptocurrency scheme that promises a large profit, and consider:

Table 1 The material conditional analysis of *if p then q*

p q	if p then q
T T	T
T F	F
F T	T
F F	T

T = true, and F = false

(3.2) If we invest in the scheme (*i*), then our money will be in honest hands (*m*).

If (3.2) were a material conditional, equivalent to *not-i or m*, its probability would increase as the probability of its antecedent, *P(i)*, decreased: *P(not-i or m)* goes up when *P(not-i)* increases. Assume we become more and more convinced, on solid grounds, that the scheme is a scam. That will make us less and less likely to invest in it, and *P(not-i)* will get higher and higher. However, that will increase *P(not-i or m)*, the probability of the material conditional, so our belief in the conditional is apparently strengthened by our reluctance to invest! Much more plausible psychologically is that we refuse to invest in the scheme because the probability of (3.2) gets lower and lower, as it will if we follow the Equation of 2.6, making *P(if i then m)* = *P(m|i)*. We will return to the Equation in Section 5 and explain how it is generally supported by psychological experiments.

Problems with the material conditional analysis eventually brought about a radical revision (beginning with Johnson-Laird et al., 2015) of mental model theory, in which the paradoxes are no longer claimed to be logically valid (see Over, 2023a, for critical comments on the revision). Williamson (2020) has a much more sophisticated defence of the material conditional analysis. It has also been criticised (Rothschild, 2023; van Rooij et al., 2023), but Williamson stresses the role of suppositions in assessing conditionals, rightly in our view given the psychological evidence. We introduced some of this evidence in Section 2.6 and will come to more of it in Section 5.

3.2 Logically Valid Reasoning and Probability

Before the development of the new paradigm, psychologists did sometimes link valid deductive reasoning and probability judgements. This link is most strongly found in the famous Tversky and Kahneman (1983) article on the *conjunction fallacy*, reporting that people sometimes judge the probability of a conjunction, *P(p & q)*, to be higher than the probability of one of its conjuncts, *P(p)*. As background for their experiments, Tversky and Kahneman pointed out that *P(p & q)* cannot be greater than *P(p)* in normative probability theory. If *p & q* could be more probable than *p*, then *p* could be false when *p & q* was true, and that is logically impossible.

More generally and considering only probability assignments that are consistent with probability theory, that have *coherence*, we can state that a one-premise inference is logically valid if and only if the probability of its premise cannot be greater than the probability of its conclusion by probability theory. For example, the natural deduction inference rule of and-elimination, *p & q* therefore *p*, is valid in probability logic as well as classical logic because $P(p \& q) \leq P(p)$. Probabilistic validity preserves probability, just as classical validity preserves truth. For inferences with more than one premise, we need to define the *uncertainty* of a premise *p* as $1 - P(p)$ and of a premise *if p then q* as $1 - P(q|p)$, and then an inference is *probabilistically valid, p-valid*, if and only if the uncertainty of its conclusion cannot exceed the sum of the uncertainties of its premises (Adams, 1998). More informally, a valid inference cannot increase our uncertainty: it cannot take us from less uncertainty to more uncertainty. An example of a two-premise inference is *and-introduction*, inferring *p & q* from *p* and *q* as separate premises. This inference is clearly classically valid, since its conclusion cannot be false when its premises are true, and p-valid, because its conclusion cannot be more uncertain than its premises. This definition of probabilistic validity, p-validity, plays a fundamental role in probability logic (Adams, 1998) and in new paradigm psychology of reasoning (Oaksford & Charter, 2020; Over, 2020).

In the traditional paradigm, reviewed in Section 2, psychologists usually asked their participants to assume the truth of the premises in a reasoning experiment while setting aside any relevant beliefs they might have. These premises could sometimes be highly abstract and were usually detached from belief acquisition, practical decision-making, or scientific prediction, and could be unbelievable when they were not abstract. Such premises are of little use in everyday or scientific reasoning, where there is little or no point in arbitrarily assuming what is irrelevant and unbelievable. Participants could find it hard to make such assumptions and could automatically use what they judged to be relevant beliefs for their inferences, with the result that they could be charged with belief bias in a traditional approach. Using a *reductio ad absurdum* argument, people do assume what they disbelieve, to try to derive an explicit absurdity from it, but usually in ordinary reasoning, this inference form relies on background beliefs and has the goal of refuting an opponent with the implicitly absurd belief. The new paradigm psychology of reasoning is in the truly psychological business of studying inferences from beliefs and relevant hypothetical suppositions. The aim is to understand and explain people's inferences, from their mostly less than certain degrees of belief in the premises, to degrees of belief in the conclusions (Cruz, 2020; Evans et al., 2015).

For instance, suppose we ask some friends of ours whether they will join us in the investment referred to in (3.2): 'If we invest in the scheme (*i*), then our money will be in honest hands (*m*)'. They might reject this possibility out of hand because $P(m|i)$ is very low for them. This belief could be so strong in them that they would resist a psychologist's request to assume that (3.2) is true for the purpose of discovering whether they endorse MP as a valid inference. But in the new paradigm, we can test whether people comply with MP by asking for their judgement about $P(m|i)$. Suppose they judge that $P(m|i) = .01$, and that they are prepared, for the purpose of relevant decision-making, to assume that $P(i) = 1$. Then as long as their judgement about the probability of the MP conclusion, $P(m)$, is not below .01, they have complied with the p-validity of MP, and there can be no justification for charging them with a bias.

The new paradigm does not exonerate reasoners from all cognitive biases. People can still have belief bias (Section 5.2) and other biases. They sometimes judge $P(p \& q) > P(p)$ even when p is *explicitly inferred* from $p \& q$ (Cruz et al., 2015). Evans et al. (2015) asked participants to assign probabilities to the premises and conclusions of conditional arguments and found that they conformed to p-validity at above chance levels, but that they do so better when premises and conclusions are grouped together as explicit inferences rather than judged separately. We get a much fairer assessment of whether people conform to logical and probabilistic principles, avoiding biases and fallacies, by studying their degrees of belief in the new paradigm.

3.3 Interpretations of Probability

There are different interpretations of probability theory (Howson & Urbach, 2006). In subjective interpretations, probability judgements are the expression of subjective degrees of belief. In objective interpretations, probability judgements describe a feature of the world – frequencies, proportions, or propensities. The new paradigm in the psychology of reasoning is grounded in the normative theories of de Finetti (1936/1995, 1937/1964) and Ramsey (1926/1990. De Finetti had only a subjective interpretation of probability, but Ramsey argued that both interpretations, subjective and objective, are necessary to cover all the uses of probability theory. In this respect, most new paradigm psychologists, including ourselves, side with Ramsey and not de Finetti.

Both authors argued, however, that people's degrees of belief can be measured by the bets they are willing to make, and both made use of the notion of a *conditional bet*, for example, we might say that, *if* a certain coin is spun, we bet it will come up heads. For this bet, suppose we observe that the coin has a worn edge and decide that we will pay 60 Euro cents to make the bet under the following conditions. We will win the bet and get 1 Euro when the outcome turns out to be heads and will lose the bet and get nothing when the outcome turns out to be tails. If the coin is not spun, the bet, being only conditional, is 'void', and we get our 60 cents back. The conditional subjective probability for us is then .60 that a head will be the result given that the worn coin is spun, and .60 is the *expected value* of the bet. Section 5.1 has more on the relation between conditional bets and the use of natural language conditionals.

We could use a heuristic, for example, the *representativeness heuristic* of Tversky and Kahneman (1983), for making our bet in another example. The person supplying and spinning the coin may appear to us to be representative, that is, highly similar to our image, of a confidence trickster. He looks shady to us and is called 'Doc' (our image being formed by films about confidence tricksters). With this heuristic giving us the belief that the coin is biased, some normative theorists might charge us with irrationality in this case. But theorists with a subjective interpretation of probability would not care whether we acquired our degrees of belief using heuristics. They would only ask if these degrees conformed to probability theory. De Finetti (1936/1995) said that he was specifying *the logic of probability*, and Ramsey's (1926/1990) phrase was *the logic of partial belief.* Hence, to have a subjective interpretation of probability is *not* to allow people to have any degrees of belief that they like. The degrees are constrained by the logic of probability and partial belief, and consistency with probability theory, coherence, is fundamental to it.

Why should we care about being coherent and conforming to probability logic? The answer given by both de Finetti and Ramsey is that, if we violate the principles of probability theory, a *Dutch book* can be made against us. This a series of bets which, if we make them, will guarantee an overall loss (Howson & Urbach, 2006). One could ask whether ordinary people are worried, implicitly, about Dutch books being made against them, but it seems highly likely that people would revise their bets to escape a Dutch book if they became aware of being caught in one. Gamblers play roulette, for example, when they know the odds are against them, but playing when it becomes clear that the roulette wheel is rigged, and they will *necessarily* lose, is quite another matter.

Implicitly using the representative heuristic, we might judge that people are more likely to be confidence tricksters and called 'Doc' than they are to be called 'Doc'. Now this judgement does violate probability theory and its logic. As a result, we have committed Tversky and Kahneman's conjunction fallacy and are incoherent, and it is possible to make a Dutch book against us (as Gilio & Over, 2012, illustrate). The concept of coherence includes classical logical consistency as a special case. It is inconsistent to imagine that $p \& q$ is true and p is false, and it is incoherent to hold that $P(p \& q) = 1$ and $P(p) = 0$. More generally, and extending binary classical logic, it is p-valid to infer p from $p \& q$ and logically incoherent to claim that $P(p \& q) > P(p)$.

We become vulnerable to Dutch books if we violate p-validity and consequently are incoherent in our reasoning. But it is impossible for human beings to certain that they are logically coherent. $P(q|p)$ must be 1 by the logic of probability when p logically implies q, and the question of whether or not p logically implies q can be computationally too hard for human beings to answer in elementary logic, and it is not always a logically decidable question in more advanced logic. Section 7 will focus on rationality and the relationship that it has to coherence, defined as consistency with probability theory. But in Section, 3.4, we will introduce a theorem of probability theory that is the starting point of the Bayesian account of how to change degrees of belief.

3.4 Bayesian Reasoning

People use *static* reasoning to extend their degrees of belief beyond their premises, but they also change their degrees of belief in a process of *belief revision* or *updating*. Reasoning to change beliefs has been called *dynamic reasoning* (Oaksford & Chater, 2020). Let us say that we have a degree of belief at time 1 in a hypothesis *h*, $P_1(h)$, but are interested in running an experiment to produce some evidence, *e*, at time 2 to enable us to update our degree of belief in *h* to $P_2(h)$. To make this update as Bayesians, we need a subjective conditional probability judgement about *h* given *e*, $P_1(h|e)$, at time 1, and we derive $P_1(h|e)$ in the following way. By probability theory, when $P_1(e)$ is not 0, $P_1(h|e)$ is $P_1(e \& h)$ divided by $P_1(e)$, formally $P_1(e \& h)/P_1(e)$. By probability theory again, $P_1(e \& h) = P_1(h)P_1(e|h)$, and so we have:

$$P_1(h|e) = P_1(e \& h)/P_1(e) = (P_1(h)P_1(e|h))/P_1(e)$$

As *e* is logically equivalent to *(h & e) or (not-h & e)*, we can derive in probability theory *the total probability theorem* that

$$P_1(e) = P_1((h \& e) \text{ or } (not\text{-}h \& e)) = P_1(h)P_1(e/h) + P_1(not\text{-}h)P_1(e/not\text{-}h)$$

and the following form of *Bayes' theorem*:

$$P_1(h|e) = (P_1(h)P_1(e|h))/(P_1(h)P_1(e/h) + P_1(not\text{-}h)P_1(e/not\text{-}h))$$

The derivation of this theorem is thus an exercise in deductive reasoning from the axioms of probability theory, and it is incoherent to violate it. But the theorem is the basis for going beyond logic and deduction in a Bayesian account of updating beliefs in a dynamic process. More formally, this updating is to go from $P_1(h)$ to $P_2(h)$ in light of new evidence *e* that has been acquired.

A special case of Bayes' theorem is when is it is logically valid to infer *e* from *h*, implying that $P_1(e|h) = 1$. In this case, if *not-e* is the result of an experiment, our hypothesis has been *falsified*, and our degree of belief $P_1(h)$ ought to be revised to become $P_2(h) = 0$ at time 2. Bayesians can use this instance of the theorem to interpret Popper's (1959) method of *falsifiability* in science. For Popper the only legitimate scientific method is to use classical logic to derive a prediction from a hypothesis. If the prediction turns out to be false, that is decisive evidence against the hypothesis. Popper's philosophy of science had a far-reaching impact on traditional psychology of reasoning (Wason & Johnson-Laird, 1972), but there are serious problems with its narrow focus on falsifying hypotheses, to the exclusion of confirmation, in the philosophy of science and psychological research (Evans, 2007a; Howson & Urbach, 2006). After long careers in the experimental study of reasoning, we testify how difficult it can be to falsify psychological theories definitively. These can be modified in the face of negative results and yet, sometimes, claimed to be the same theory.

Bayesians use Bayes' theorem in an account of belief change that is more general than Popper's. It allows for the confirmation, as well as disconfirmation (itself wider than falsification), of hypotheses and general belief revision and updating (Howson & Urbach, 2006; Sprenger & Hartmann, 2019). The theorem can give us a value for $P_1(h|e)$, supposing we can make judgements about $P_1(h)$, noting that $P_1(not\text{-}h) = 1 - P_1(h)$, and the *likelihoods* $P_1(e|h)$ and $P_1(e|not\text{-}h)$. Assume an experiment is conducted, or an observation is made, and new information becomes available that e holds at time 2, $P_2(e) = 1$. We can then use *Bayesian strict conditionalisation* to update our *prior* degree of belief in h, $P_1(h)$, to a new *posterior* degree of belief, $P_2(h) = P_1(h|e)$, provided that $P_1(h|e)$ is *invariant*: $P_1(h|e) = P_2(h|e)$. Invariance holds when learning the new information e does not also lead to a change in relevant conditional probability judgements. As we have noted, the proof of Bayes' theorem is a deduction from the axioms of probability theory, and it would be logically incoherent to give some other value to $P_1(h|e)$. However, a judgement that invariance holds, $P_1(h|e) = P_2(h|e)$, can go beyond deductive logic, and it is not necessarily logically incoherent to infer that invariance does not hold in some contexts.

For a simple example of strict conditionalisation, suppose there are two coins, one double-head and one fair. Let one of these coins be selected at random and h be the hypothesis that the selected coin is the double-headed one. Suppose the coin is spun and clearly comes up heads. As Bayesians, we can reason in the following way. Before the spinning, we judge $P_1(h) = P_1(not\text{-}h) = .5$. With he as the evidence the coin comes up heads, $P_1(he|h) = 1$ and $P_1(he|not\text{-}h) = .5$. In this special case. Bayes' theorem implies that $P_1(h|he) = .5/.75 = .66$. When the coin comes up heads, he, we can finally conclude that $P_2(h) = .66$ using strict Bayesian conditionalisation. This dynamic reasoning process has given us a higher degree of belief that the selected coin is the double-headed one.

Not even this simple example can be a purely deductive exercise about coherence. We have inferred, at least implicitly, that the probability the coin will end its spin on its edge, and not with a head or tail, is negligible, but that may not be so for this particular coin. We have also effectively presupposed invariance. If we learn, not only that *he* holds, but that a sleight of hand trick substituted a double-tailed coin for the fair one before the random selection, then invariance will not hold, and we will conclude that $P_2(h) = 1$. Non-deductive inferences, the topic of Section 4, are present even in this rudimentary example.

For a less artificial example, recall our earlier statement:

(3.1) If Arthur is in Edinburgh (*d*), then Carol is in Glasgow (*g*).

Assume we have a modest degree of belief that Arthur is in Edinburgh. We could try to falsify it by going to Edinburgh to look for Arthur. The problem is that we could search for him indefinitely if he is not there. But suppose we have a high degree of confidence that (3.1) holds, making $P_1(g|d)$ high for us via the Equation, and we have a low degree of belief that Carol is in Glasgow given Arthur is not in Edinburgh, making $P_1(g|not\text{-}d)$ low for us. Though P_1 *(d)* may be at a middling value for us, we can use Bayes' theorem to infer that $P_1(d|g)$ is quite high. At this point, if we discover that Carol is definitely in Glasgow, $P_2(g) = 1$, and we are quite confident that invariance holds, we can use strict conditionalisation to increase our confidence that Arthur is in Edinburgh, $P_2(d) > P_1(d)$.

In strict conditionalisation, we are certain of the evidence, and it can be thought of, given the Equation, as *dynamic* MP, inferring a new degree of belief in *q* from a degree of belief in *if p then q* after learning that *p* certainly holds. Other inferences, like MT, have dynamic, belief-changing forms as well. But invariance can more easily fail for MT than MP. Consider:

(3.3) If Arthur is not in Edinburgh, then he is in Scotland.

We might have a high degree of belief in (3.3) because we know that Arthur was going to catch the London train to Edinburgh but, by the train times, might be just short of Edinburgh. If we learn, however, that Arthur is not in Scotland as a result of missing his train in London, we will not appeal to (3.3) and conclude, using MT and double negation (inferring *p* from *not-not-p*), that he is in Edinburgh. It will be clear to us that invariance has failed and that (3.3) has a probability of 0. We saw in Section 2.4 that, although MP and MT are both valid inferences in classical and probability logic, the endorsement frequency of MT is significantly lower than that of MP. Whether this fact can be explained by some awareness of the greater fragility of dynamic MT is yet to be explored in the psychology of reasoning.

Strict conditionalisation is called 'strict' because we use it when we are certain of the evidence. But perhaps there is some uncertainty about whether Carol is in Glasgow, and so we cannot increase $P_2(g)$ to 1. Let us suppose we can increase $P_2(g)$, so that $P_2(g) > P_1(g)$. In this case, we can use a more general Bayesian procedure than strict conditionalisation to go from the prior to the posterior, $P_1(d) < P_2(d)$. This procedure is *Jeffrey conditionalisation* (Jeffrey, 1983, Ch. 11):

$$P_2(d) = P_2(g)P_1(d|g) + P_2(not\text{-}g)P_1(d|not\text{-}g)$$

Invariance, $P_2(d|g) = P_1(d|g)$ and $P_2(d|not\text{-}g) = P_1(d|not\text{-}g)$, is again assumed here. In our example, the probability that Arthur is in Edinburgh is determined by the probability that Carol is in Glasgow and what that tells us about the probability that Arthur in Edinburgh plus the probability that Carol is not in Glasgow and what that tells us about the probability that Arthur in Edinburgh (for Arthur might be in Edinburgh even if Carol is not in Glasgow).

Jeffrey conditionalisation can be thought of as dynamic MP from an uncertain minor premise, but some experimental results imply that people do not always conform precisely to it (Hadjichristidis et al., 2014; Zhao & Osherson, 2010). They may focus on only one conditional component, $P_1(d|g)$ or $P_1(d|not\text{-}g)$. This is implied by the descriptive *singularity principle*, the psychological hypothesis that people tend to simplify, as a default, their reasoning by focusing on only one hypothetical possibility at a time. There is much psychological evidence for this principle (see Evans, 2006, 2007a). Such singular focus, however, does not necessarily imply that they are incoherent. It could be coherent for them to presuppose, for example, that $P_1(d|not\text{-}g) = 0$ in some contexts.

3.5 Diagnosticity

In our example of Bayesian reasoning about Arthur and Carol, we took the antecedent of (3.1), d, as the hypothesis, and its consequent, g, as the evidence, and as we have just explained, the singularity principle implies that people might tend to focus on $P_1(d|g)$ in Jeffrey conditionalisation and to ignore $P_1(d|not\text{-}g)$. This principle implies as well that, in the use of Bayes' theorem at the start of this reasoning process, people might tend to concentrate on $P_1(g|d)$ and to ignore $P_1(g|not\text{-}d)$, which could actually be higher than $P_1(g|d)$. They might tend to rely only on the evidence given the hypothesis, $P_1(e|h)$, when they should be conforming fully to Bayes' theorem, which requires them to take the evidence given the negation of the hypothesis, $P_1(e|not\text{-}h)$, into account as well. There is, indeed, some support for this conclusion in experimental studies.

By Bayes' theorem, e has variable *diagnosticity*, with $P_1(h|e)$ increasing as $P_1(e|h)$ increases and $P_1(e|not\text{-}h)$ decreases. The *likelihood ratio* compares $P_1(e|h)$ with $P_1(e|not\text{-}h)$, and people should, at least implicitly, make use of it to comply fully with the theorem. But beginning with Doherty et al. (1979), psychologists have found that participants in studies can prefer information only relevant to assessing $P_1(e|h)$, while ignoring possible information relevant to $P_1(e|not\text{-}h)$, or to a number of possible hypotheses that are reasonable alternatives to h. Their participants tended to focus on a favoured hypothesis and to seek only confirmation of it. In technical terms, they reasoned *pseudo-diagnostically* and had a *confirmation bias*.

However, information on $P_1(e|h)$ can be more available than information about $P_1(e|not\text{-}h)$. We may often have experienced a cough as a symptom of a common cold but have no knowledge of its frequency when people have some kind of new viral infection, and it could be hard to find that out. But in some contexts, as we have pointed out, it is logically coherent to assume to that $P_1(e|not\text{-}h)$ is 0. It could be coherent, with certain background beliefs, to infer that there is 0 probability Carol is in Glasgow given Arthur is not in Edinburgh. Research following Doherty et al. (1979) has presented a more complex, and less negative, picture of people's diagnostic reasoning, but those results continue to be consistent with the singularity principle that people tend as a default to focus their reasoning on a single hypothesis (Evans, 2006, 2007a).

3.6 Conclusion

In recent years, most psychologists have abandoned the traditional paradigm view that the conditional in natural language is a material conditional when people fully model its meaning. Surprisingly for a psychological paradigm, the traditional approach paid little attention to inferences from beliefs, except as a biasing factor, and made no attempt at all to explain changes in degrees of belief. In contrast, the new paradigm focuses on the connection between reasoning and degrees of belief and changes in degrees of belief. There is more to reasoning from degrees of belief and belief change than deductive inferences in probability theory. There are non-deductive inferences and strict and Jeffrey conditionalisation with inferences about invariance. However, the new paradigm does not expect people to be perfectly in line with any normative principles, with no simplifying cognitive processes, or for their degrees of belief always to match objective probabilities. It does expect to provide a better scientific account of people's reasoning by studying their degrees of belief and how these change over time.

4 Non-deductive Reasoning

We introduced Bayesian reasoning in Section 3.4 and explained that the proof of Bayes' theorem is itself an instance of deductive reasoning from the axioms of probability theory. That it is the starting point for Bayesian accounts of non-deductive reasoning, resulting in belief updating using strict or Jeffrey conditionalisation when invariance holds. Deductive reasoning by itself cannot give us a full account of belief change, and the traditional deductive paradigm had nothing to say about updating degrees of belief. In this section, we discuss in detail more examples of how human reasoning has to go beyond deduction, to select hypotheses to test and to make inferences that are not deductive.

4.1 Wason's 2–4–6 Task

Wason (1960) introduced the *2–4–6 task* as an experiment on whether people try to falsify hypotheses, as Popper would recommend (see Evans, 2016, for detailed review of psychological work with this task). It is also an illustration of the importance of selecting hypotheses to test and of not focusing on a single hypothesis. Wason told his participants that he had a mind a rule for generating whole number triples, and he gave them an example of a triple that conformed to his rule: 2–4–6. He asked them to try to discover his rule by producing a new triple themselves and asking him whether it conformed to his rule. He would answer 'Yes' or 'No'. After receiving his answer, they were able to choose another triple, and the process would continue. He asked them as well to write down their reasons for selecting their triples as guesses and to state the rule when they thought they knew it.

Wason's hidden rule was that any ascending sequence was acceptable, and it is intuitive that most people would not think of this rule as their first hypothesis about what Wason had in mind. What many appeared to do was to jump to the conclusion that the rule was to 'increase the three numbers by two' or at least by equal intervals, and they typically asked about three numbers consistent with their hypothesis, for example, 5 7 9, in a *positive test* strategy. In such case they would invariably receive a 'Yes' response, appearing to confirm their hypothesis. The participants did not seem to Wason to be trying to falsify the hypotheses that they considered. They could additionally be said to have assigned too high a prior probability, $P_1(h)$, to the hypothesis that appeared to be suggested by the context.

Influenced by Popper and helping to initiate the traditional paradigm, Wason inferred that his participants had a serious failing in rationality. When Wason and Johnson-Laird (1972) reviewed the 2–4–6 task, they charged the participants with having a confirmation bias, the tendency to seek verification in the task and not falsification. They pointed out that a negative test of their hypothesis, such as 1 5 6 would have falsified it. But the problem is that, in general, positive testing can lead to falsification of hypotheses and is frequently used in science as well as normal life (see Evans, 1989, 2016). If one predicts an experimental result that is not observed, that is a falsification. Hence, one cannot infer a *confirmatory attitude* simply from the observation of positive testing, as a number of later authors have noted. The difficulty of the 2–4–6 task arises from the fact that the participant is cued by the biased example to adopt a hypothesis which is a more specific case of the actual rule of any ascending sequence. In this particular situation, all positive tests will get positive feedback. The hypothesis is not so much incorrect as insufficiently general. Their mistake is like stating, truly, that iron expands when heated, without testing if this property applies to metals in general.

Consider a Bayesian analysis of this task in the new paradigm. Because of the way it is presented to them, the participants may assign a high prior probability that Wason's hidden rule was that to increase the three numbers by two. Letting this hypothesis be *ht*, their implicit judgement was that $P_1(ht)$ was high at the start of the task. The conditional probability of a 'Yes' answer, *y*, given *ht* and the use of 5 7 9 as a guess is 1, for *y* can be logically deduced from *ht* and the use of 5 7 9. Let us just express this judgement as $P_1(y|ht) = 1$, with the understanding that it has made in the context of 5 7 9 as the guess. The participants might have been so focused on their hypothesis *ht* that they made no judgement about the probability of *y* given its negation, $P_1(y|not\text{-}ht)$, but it is clear that a 'No', *not-y*, reply to 5 7 9 should result, by strict conditionalisation, in a posterior judgement that *ht* was certainly false, $P_2(ht) = 0$, as $P_1(not\text{-}y|ht)$ should be 0 when $P_1(y|ht)$ is 1. The hypothesis would be falsified, and a high degree of prior belief in it should fall to 0. A 'Yes' answer would confirm *ht* in a Bayesian analysis, increasing the degree of belief in it, in this positive test strategy. A *negative test strategy* would be to guess a triple that should receive a 'No' answer given the hypothesis, like 1 2 3. With the understanding that this triple is the guess, $P_1(not\text{-}y|ht) = 1$, and then falsification, from a 'Yes' reply, or confirmation, from a 'No' reply, could again result.

More precision in a Bayesian analysis of the task is impossible when $P_1(ht)$ and $P_1(y|not\text{-}ht)$ are not specified. At Wason's suggestion, some studies of it did eventually help participants to think about both a hypothesis, *ht*, and its negation, *not-ht*, or an instance of its negation, with *dual goal* instructions (Evans, 2016). This resulted in much higher solution rates on the 2–4–6 task, although participants still followed a positive test strategy for a complementary hypothesis which was only implicitly negative for the focal hypothesis. Note that a negative test strategy is not normally needed, or even advantageous, in many contexts (see Klayman & Ha, 1987; Poletiek, 2001). In a fully Bayesian and new paradigm version of the task, the participants' judgements $P_1(ht)$ and $P_1(y|not\text{-}ht)$ would have to be measured, and the question would be how closely their posterior judgement would be to the $P_2(ht)$ that was implied by Bayes' theorem and conditionalisation. But the existing studies do support the implication of the singularity principle (Evans, 2007a): that people will tend to focus on a single hypothesis that is of importance to them, until they have a reason to give it up. This is also consistent with the *cognitive miser* hypothesis (Stanovich, 2018), positing a system which evolved to minimise cognitive effort.

Of course, conforming to probability theory and being logically coherent are not enough for effective reasoning and belief updating in the real world. People must not only go beyond probability theory by using strict or Jeffrey conditionalisation and making inferences about invariance. They must also have a strategy for considering hypotheses and updating them. There is no proof in probability theory that obliges us, on pain of incoherence, to have a positive or negative test strategy or some combination of the two. Someone could be logically coherent forever by asking Wason about numbers that increased by two.

There are then lessons to be learned from Wason's 2–4–6 task, but it can still be argued that it does not correspond well to scientific investigations of hypotheses or to most ordinary belief updating. It could be charged that it is artificial for people to have to trust someone to tell them whether a hidden rule had been conformed to by some data. But we do have to depend in ordinary reasoning on experts to tell us what has been confirmed and well established. We face too many complex questions and problems in our contemporary world, even in our everyday reasoning and decision-making, to rely only on whatever highly limited expertise we may possess (see Sloman & Fernbach, 2017, on how we 'never think alone'). Even if we derive $P_1(h|e)$ using Bayes' theorem, we may well have to trust an expert to tell us that e holds and concluding that someone is trustworthy has to be mainly the result of non-deductive reasoning. In the next section, we will introduce experiments on relying on experts in arguments.

4.2 Argumentation

The study of *argumentation* in psychology seeks to account for people's informal and ordinary use of arguments in reasoning (Hahn & Oaksford, 2007; Oaksford & Chater, 2020). Many common arguments are deductively valid, with both classical and p-validity. The best example is simply MP, which is so common, and often so automatic, that its use can pass unnoticed. But the premises of MP and other valid inferences usually have to be supported by arguments that are not deductively valid. A Bayesian new paradigm approach reveals that some of these invalid inferences can be strong, well-justified reasoning in some contexts, with highly probable conclusions, and not the unqualified 'fallacies' of a traditional classification. For example, the classical fallacy of Affirmation of the Consequent (AC), inferring *h* from *if h then e* and *e*, is classically invalid and p-invalid, but it can sometimes be given a straightforward justification using Bayes' theorem and conditionalisation, leading to updating of the degree of belief in *h*.

One way we all have to simplify and widen our reasoning is by relying on experts to a large extent. To decide whether to take Ivermectin to try to prevent COVID-19, we cannot run the relevant scientific experiments ourselves but must try to identify the appropriate experts who are also trustworthy. Harris et al. (2016) studied what was sometimes classically called the *appeal to authority* argument. This argument form is clearly logically invalid. Relying on even a well-qualified and honest authority can lead to false beliefs. But Harris et al. (2016) proposed a Bayesian model of this form and considered the conditional probability that a hypothesis will be asserted by an expert given that it holds, $P_1(h_a|h)$, as we will symbolise it here. If $P_1(h_a|h)$ is much greater than $P_1(h_a|not\text{-}h)$, that is, the likelihood ratio is high, and our prior probability judgement for *h*, $P_1(h)$, is also not very low, then $P_1(h|h_a)$, the probability that *h* holds given that the possible expert has asserted it, will be relatively high, and this 'appeal to authority' argument will be a relatively strong one, leading to a higher posterior degree of belief in *h*, $P_2(h)$, when the expert does assert *h*, that is, h_a holds.

To refine their Bayesian model, Harris et al. introduced the expertise, *ex*, and the trustworthiness, *tr*, of the supposed expert who asserts the hypothesis as factors in a Bayesian analysis of this argument form. All the relevant conditional probabilities are represented, e.g., $P_1(h_a|h \ \& \ ex \ \& \ tr)$ is the conditional probability that the hypothesis is asserted given that it holds, that the asserter is an expert, and that the asserter is trustworthy. The model is simplified by assuming that *h*, *ex*, and *tr* are independent of each other. Independence, and conditional independence, assumptions are of importance in simplifying Bayesian models. In this instance, the independence assumption allows Harris et al. to predict what the $P_1(h|h_a)$ judgements should be, according to the model, from judgements about $P_1(h_a|h \ \& \ ex \ \& \ tr)$ and the other relevant probabilities. Their two experiments gave good, though somewhat noisy, support to their model.

This model is computational, as Harris et al. emphasise. They do not try to give an account of the underlying psychological processes. These may be relatively simple in some cases. We might believe that, if Ivermectin is not effective for treating COVID-19, then the USA Food and Drug Administration (FDA) will not approve it for treating COVID-19, and infer from this that, if the FDA does not approve it for treating COVID-19, then it is not effective for treating COVID-19. Inferring high confidence in *if p then q* from high confidence in *if q then* p can be a strong inference in some contexts (justified by Bayes' theorem). We might infer that the FDA gives expert advice because it is similar to the European Medicines Agency (EMA), and we already believe that the EMA gives expert advice (see Feeney, 2018, on this kind of inference based on similarity). There are always many questions for psychologists to answer to complete Bayesian computational theories of reasoning.

4.3 Base Rates and Natural Sampling

In spite of the successes of Bayesian computational models (Oaksford & Chater, 2020), there is reason to think that it can sometimes be difficult for people to use Bayesian reasoning. Suppose that participants in a study are given the following Bayesian problem:

> There is a .02 probability that a medical expert will be picked out from a group in a certain context, $P_1(h_{mex}) = .02$. The probability is 1 the person picked out will state that Veklury can be an effective treatment for COVID-19 if they are a medical expert, $P_1(h_{sv}|h_{mex}) = 1$, and a probability of .5 that the picked out person will state Veklury can be an effective treatment for COVID-19 if they are not a medical expert, $P_1(h_{sv}|not\text{-}h_{mex}) = .5$. What is the probably the person is a medical expert if they state that Veklury can be an effective treatment for COVID-19, $P_1(h_{mex}|h_{sv})$?

The correct answer to the above question, using Bayes' theorem, is about .04, that is, $P_1(h_{mex}|h_{sv})$ is about .04. Studies of problems like the above have been run for a long time, following on from Tversky & Kahneman (1974), and it has been found that participants tend not to answer them correctly, responding that $P_1(h_{mex}|h_{sv})$ is much higher than .04. They seem to be suffering from the fallacy of *base-rate neglect*. In above example, this fallacy would be not to take account, or insufficient account, of the fact that the prior probability, the *base rate*, that the person picked out is a medical expert is so low, with $P_1(h_{mex}) = .02$. It is true that medical experts will apparently make the statement about Veklury with certainty, and the non-experts will respond with this statement at random, but there are many more non-experts than experts in this sample, and there will be many more statements made about Veklury as an effective treatment for COVID-19 by non-experts than by experts. The fact that someone makes this statement will therefore not be strong evidence that they are a medical expert.

Influenced by Kleiter (1994), Gigerenzer and Hoffrage (1995) found that Bayesian reasoning can be improved if experimenters use what they called *natural frequencies* in the Bayesian word problems given to their participants.

For the above problem, a *natural sampling* (Kleiter, 1994) version using natural frequencies would go like this:

> In a sample of 100 people, 2 are medical experts and 98 are not medical experts. The two who are medical experts will state that Veklury can be an effective treatment for COVID-19. Out of the 98 who are not medical experts, 49 will state that Veklury can be an effective treatment for COVID-19. Out of all those who state that Veklury can be an effective treatment for COVID-19 how many will be medical experts, ___ out of ___?

The correct answer to this problem is 2 out of 51, and it is clearly easier for most people to come by than .04, or more accurately .039, or an even more accurate longer decimal expansion. Cosmides and Tooby (1996) used an evolutionary argument to try to explain why such versions of Bayesian problems are relatively easy to solve. They argued that our human ancestors, who lived as hunter-gatherers for almost all of our evolutionary history, acquired, by natural selection, an adaptive dedicated module for easily processing 'natural frequencies'. For example, hunter-gatherers might, arguably, have concluded that 47 out of 52 of their group members who ate a certain red berry recovered from a cold within a week.

We doubt that an evolutionary hypothesis about a dedicated module for natural sampling can explain how a 'natural frequency' format facilitates Bayesian reasoning in a psychological word problem (see Evans, 2007a and Over, 2003). Even if a group of hunter-gatherers had the linguistic means to represent a number like 47 or 52, this sample from their group might well not tell them that eating the red berry explains a recovery in a week (Sebben & Ullrich, 2021). The sample could be biased, and even if it is not, people may recover from a cold within a week whether they eat the berry or not.

The term 'natural frequency' suggests that there is an objective frequency in play here. But natural sampling only gives us *sample frequencies*, which must be processed further in non-deductive reasoning for high degrees of confidence in objective frequencies and causes. Bayesian belief updating, with its non-deductive aspects, is itself needed to take us from a sample frequency of, for instance, five heads in a row to a high degree of confidence that a coin has a bias which results in a high objective probability of coming up heads.

We do not doubt, of course, that hunter-gatherers inferred the existence of some objective frequencies and causes through non-deductive reasoning that increased their reproductive success. They could notice that there was rapid new berry and other growth that attracted game after a fire cleared a forest. They apparently started fires themselves for this purpose for tens of thousands of years (Zimmer, 2021). These *interventions* could have, in effect, confirmed for them a Bayesian model for such causal reasoning (Pearl, 2000; Sloman & Lagnado, 2015). Some simple natural sampling would have played a part in this process. Still, solving a word problem in a psychological experiment is a long way from starting fires to encourage the growth of blueberries, and a dedicated module for natural sampling could help with the latter, but not the former.

For us, Tversky and Kahneman (1983) had the key insight for explaining why participants in psychological experiments can solve Bayesian word problems when these are in a 'natural frequency' format. In their article, as we have reported in Section 3.2, they found that people sometimes commit the conjunction fallacy of, for example, judging that it is more probable than a man is over 55 and has had one or more heart attacks than that the man has had one or more heart attacks. But they also found that instances of this fallacy significantly decreased when it was expressed using sample frequencies. In one study, they told their participants that there was a sample of 100 males, asked how many of these 100 men had one or more heart attacks, and how many of these 100 men both were over 55 years and had had one or more heart attacks. Given these questions, we would avoid the conjunction fallacy by replying, for example, that 10 of these 100 men had had one or more heart attacks and that 8 of these had had 1 or more heart attacks and were over 55. Tversky and Kahneman pointed out that, in this version of the task, the class inclusion relation can be 'readily perceived and appreciated'. The class of men who have had one or more heart attacks and are over 55 is necessarily included in the class of men who have had one or more heart attacks, and this relationship can be literally seen when we draw *Euler circles* in which the circle for former class is inside the circle for the latter class (Barbey & Sloman, 2007).

In mathematical set theory, when one class includes another, the latter is also said to be a subset of the former, and we can say that, when this relation holds, the subset and the set that includes it are 'nested', as Euler circles can be nested. The *nested-sets hypothesis* implies that a nested-sets format is what helps people to answer questions about sample frequencies, avoiding the conjunction fallacy and base-rate neglect. This hypothesis has been confirmed in many studies (Barbey & Sloman, 2007). The natural sampling format puts its samples in a nest-sets relationship, and it now seems to be generally accepted that a 'natural frequency' problem has to have a nested-sets structure to be trivially easy to solve (McDowell & Jacobs, 2017).

There is a necessary connection between elementary set theory and logical relations, as we effectively illustrated when we introduced the conjunction fallacy in Section 3.2. This can be seen in the Euler circle representation of logical relations. The circle of p & q truths is inside the circle of p truths, representing the logical fact that the set of cases in which p & q is true is necessarily a subset of the cases in which p is true. Specifically, the rows of a truth table in which p & q is true is a subset of the rows of a truth table in which p is true. Making logical relations clear with a set-subset and nested-sets presentation helps people to avoid fallacies, both in classical logic and the logic of probability. When we give our participants the free gift of a nested-sets representation in an experimental word problem, they can do well. But in the real world, people do not usually receive this free gift, and then how often they do well with non-deductive reasoning about sample frequencies is a different question.

4.4 Conclusion

Effective non-deductive reasoning for reproduction, argumentation, or other goals has to be more than logical inferences about sets and subsets. This is just to repeat, in other words, that effective reasoning from degrees of belief and for belief change has to be more than deductive inferences in probability theory. There are inferences about invariance, which are usually non-deductive, to account for. And Wason's participants could have been logically coherent by naively accepting the hypothesis suggested by the context of his 2–4–6 task and asking indefinitely about triples increasing by two. Choices must be made about which hypotheses to test and how to test them. But no matter what normative principles are proposed for people's reasoning, they will have to simplify it. They can sometimes do this by trying to rely on experts, but identifying experts is sometimes itself hard for people, and they can fail miserably at it. There can be effective and efficient ways or heuristics to make inferences, but these are not perfect and can also cause problems. That must have been true even when we were in the happy state of being hunter-gatherers.

We have continued to assume in this section that the Equation, $P(if\ p\ then\ q) = P(q|p)$, holds for natural language conditionals. Deductive and non-deductive inferences from p to q, and the strength of these inferences, can be 'summed up' in *if p then q*, and in $P(q|p)$. It is now time for a fuller account of *if p then q* which implies the Equation.

5 Conditionals

The new paradigm in the psychology of reasoning identifies the probability of the natural language conditional, $P(if\ p\ then\ q)$, with the conditional subjective probability of q given p, $P(q|p)$, and aims to integrate the study of conditional reasoning with studies of subjective probability and utility judgements. The origin of the new paradigm can be traced back to de Finetti's and Ramsey's foundational studies of subjective probability (Section 3.3).

5.1 De Finetti's Conditional in Psychology

Wason (1966) found that participants in an experiment did not fully conform to the truth table for the material conditional. They agreed that *if p then q* is true when *p* is true and *q* is true and is false when *p* is true and *q* is false. But when they were given a false antecedent *not-p* case, they tended to respond that this was 'irrelevant' to assessing *if p then q* for truth and falsity. The resulting three-valued table came to be known as the 'defective' truth table in psychology (Over & Baratgin, 2017).

The new probabilistic paradigm in the psychology of reasoning has led to a strong interest in de Finetti's (1936/1995) three-valued table for his conditional and in his associated logic of subjective probability, with a third value, *u*, indicating doubt or uncertainty (see Egré et al., 2021, on de Finettian three-valued semantics). The subjective focus of de Finetti's approach makes it particularly relevant to psychology. Table 2 is the *de Finetti table* for the conditional.

In de Finetti's account, *if p then q* is judged to 'true' when *p* and *q* are known to be true, and 'false' when *p* is known to be true and *q* false. But when *p* is known to be false, de Finetti held that *if p then q* is doubtful or uncertain ('douteux' in the original French of Finetti, 1936/1995), and 'void' (to use the technical term of de Finetti, 1937/1964). There have been many logical proposals for three-valued analyses of conditionals, and these can be studied in psychological experiments to explore how far ordinary's people's judgements correspond to them (Baratgin et al., 2018). But in de Finetti's account, the third value *u* expresses doubt or uncertainty as a subjective mental state. It can be refined into a more precise conditional subjective probability judgement at a higher level of understanding (Baratgin et al., 2018; Over & Baratgin, 2017).

Skovgaard-Olsen et al. (2017) studied the 'defective' truth table and found that there were not as many 'irrelevant' or 'neither true nor false' responses as would be predicted from the de Finetti table. But they noted that the de Finetti table might do better if it were combined with the hypothesis that people

Table 2 The de Finetti Table for *if p then q*

p q	if p then q
T T	T
T F	F
F T	*u*
F F	*u*

T = true, F = false, and *u* = uncertain.

sometimes pragmatically interpret the assertion of a conditional, *if p then q*, as conveying a biconditional *p if and only if q*. For instance, people might pragmatically infer 'If the daughter became a millionaire, then she inherited all the money' from an assertion of 'If the daughter inherits all the money, then she will become a millionaire'.

As Baratgin et al. (2018) pointed out, de Finetti's third value expresses a state of subjective uncertainty and not some other vaguer notion of 'irrelevance'. They confirmed that his three-valued table does better than other proposed tables at accounting for participants' responses in experiments where there is such state of doubt, and the conditionals could not be interpreted as biconditionals. In their materials, they used round and square chips that could be black or white, with conditionals like the following about a randomly selected chip:

(5.1) If the chip is square (*s*) then it is black (*b*).

In their design, *s* and *b* could be uncertain as well as *if s then b*. The uncertainty was visual. A 'filter' made it impossible at times to tell whether or not a given chip was round or square or black or white.

A de Finetti analysis of the natural language conditional *if p then q* implies further that there is a close relation between someone's assertion of it and a conditional bet *if p then I bet that q*. It would make no real difference whether one asserted (5.1) or 'If the chip is square then I bet it is black'. The conditional bet is won when *p* and *q* are true and lost when *p* is true and *q* is false. Table 2 could equally represent a conditional bet, with T and F in the final column being 'won' and 'lost'. As we pointed out in Section 3.3 for the type of conditional bet described there, the probability it will be won is $P(q|p)$, which is its expected value. Baratgin et al. (2013) and Politzer et al. (2010) confirmed this close relationship in people' judgements.

In an extension of de Finetti's analysis, in which the third value *u* expresses uncertainty about *if p then q*, *u* becomes the conditional probability $P(q|p)$ itself (Sanfilippo et al., 2020). It is the expected value, or 'prevision' to use de

Table 3 The Jeffrey table for *if p then q*

p q	*if p then q*
T T	T
T F	F
F T	$P(q|p)$
F F	$P(q|p)$

T = true, F = false, and $P(q|p)$ = the conditional subjective probability of *q* given *p*

Finetti's term, of an assertion of the conditional. Table 3 has come to be known as the *Jeffrey table* (Jeffrey, 1991; Over & Cruz 2018, 2023) for *if p then q*. The Jeffrey table avoids a problem with the de Finetti table. The trivial logical truth *if p & q then p*, for example, should not have the value *u* when *p* is false and *u* means 'doubtful' or 'uncertain'. It should have the value 1, and $P(p|(p \& q))$ is of course 1.

The Jeffrey table combines very well with a pragmatic account of some uses of 'true' and 'false' (Adams, 1998; Over & Cruz, 2023), to complement objective interpretations of truth and falsity in the *p & q* and the *p & not-q* cases. In the pragmatic use, the assertion of *if p then q* would be termed 'true' when $P(q|p)$ at or near 1, and 'false' when $P(q|p)$ was at or near 0. With this supplementary hypothesis about pragmatic uses of 'true' and 'false', asserting that *if p then q* is 'true', or 'false', does not necessarily imply, for followers of de Finetti, that *p* is true, but only that $P(q|p)$ is high for the pragmatic context.

We introduced the Equation, *P(if p then q)* = $P(q|p)$, for the conditional in natural language, in Section 2.6. Psychologists of reasoning have highly confirmed it in experiments as the conditional probability hypothesis for people's judgements about a wide range of indicative conditionals and some counterfactuals (see the reviews by Evans & Over, 2004, Over, 2020, and Over & Cruz, 2018, 2023). Supporters of the Equation commonly combine it with the *Ramsey test* (Ramsey, 1929/1990) as a psychological process for determining *P(if p then q)*. According to this 'test', as extended by Stalnaker (1968), we are to make a judgement about *if p then q* by *supposing p* is the case, while making minimal changes to our beliefs to preserve consistency, and then judging our degree of belief in *q* under this supposition. The result is then a judgement about the conditional subjective probability of *q* given *p*, $P(q|p)$, and this is identified with *P(if p then q)*.

A conditional satisfying the Equation has been called a 'probability conditional' (Adams, 1998), and a 'conditional event' (de Finetti, 1937/1964), but in this Element we will use *suppositional conditional* as a general term for such a conditional, and *suppositional theories* (like that in Evans & Over, 2004) for accounts that imply that the Equation holds for the natural language conditional. A suppositional conditional *if p then q* can also be read informally as *q supposing p* (see Evans, 2020, on pragmatic features of a suppositional conditional). Lewis (1976) proved that a conditional *if p then q* in the bivalent and modal theories of Lewis (1973) and Stalnaker (1968) cannot generally have a probability that is equal to the conditional probability, $P(q|p)$. In other words, a Lewis or Stalnaker conditional cannot be thought of as a suppositional conditional. (See Edgington, 1995, for an intuitive account of Lewis's result, and Cantwell, 2020, for further points). The proof does not apply to de Finetti approaches, which are not bivalent (Lassiter, 2019; Sanfilippo et al., 2020).

5.2 Inferential connections

Suppositional accounts of the conditional fit perfectly into the new Bayesian paradigm in the psychology of reasoning. As we have explained in Section 3, this new approach does not restrict itself to inferences from arbitrary premises that are to be assumed true, outside of any context that makes them relevant, but focuses much more on inferences from degrees of belief to degrees of belief in static reasoning and on dynamic inferences through time leading to belief revisions or updating. We will cover static reasoning next in this section and move on to dynamic reasoning in the next.

Let us recall the definition of p-validity from Section 3.2. An inference is p-valid if and only if the uncertainty of its conclusion cannot be coherently greater than the sum the uncertainties of its premises (Adams, 1998). Consider this example as a suppositional conditional:

(5.2) If Anne invests in the cryptocurrency scheme (*a*), then Carol will too (*c*).

Suppose our degree of belief in (5.2) is $P(c|a) = .6$, and our degree of belief in *a* is $P(a) = .7$, and consider MP, inferring *c* from *if a then c* and *a*. Let us also say that, after making this inference, we judge $P(c)$ to be .6. Our degree of belief in *c*, .6, is coherent and does not violate the p-validity of MP as the uncertainty of *c*, $(1 - .6)$, is not greater than the sum of the uncertainties of the premises, $(1 - .6) + (1 - .7)$.

The paradoxes of the material conditional are prime examples of inferences that are not p-valid for suppositional conditionals. $P(q|p)$ can be low when P *(not-p)* is high, and when $P(q)$ is high, and experiments have shown that people do not at all accept these inferences as p-valid in their probability judgements (Cruz et al., 2017). The formal system for p-validity (Adams, 1998) is sometimes called System P (Gilio et al., 2020; Pfeifer & Kleiter, 2009). It descends from de Finetti's (1936/1995) logic of probability and Ramsey's (1926/1990) logic of partial belief.

As we saw in Section 3.3, coherence in the logic of probability corresponds to consistency in classical logic but is more general. It is of particular relevance in the new paradigm, as are the logical *coherence intervals* that can be derived for inferences (Pfeifer & Kleiter, 2009). A coherence interval for an inference specifies the range in which the probability of the conclusion must fall for coherence. For example, the coherence interval for MP follows from the total probability theorem:

$$P(c) = P(a)P(c|a) + P(not\text{-}a)P(c|not\text{-}a)$$

By probability theory, we know that $P(not\text{-}a) = 1 - P(a)$, but we might be unable to make a definite judgement about $P(c|not\text{-}a)$, which has to be used to determine the precise 'total' probability of c. But instead of a precise value, we can infer an interval for the probability of c. Carol may have a reason for investing in the scheme even if Anne does not invest in it, or Carol might not invest if Carol does not. In any event, $P(c|not\text{-}a)$ can have a maximum value of 1, and a minimum value of 0, by probability theory. If $P(c|not\text{-}a) = 1$, then $P(c) = P(a)P(c|a) + 1 - P(a) = (.6)(.7) + .3 = .72$. If $P(c|not\text{-}a) = 0$, then $P(c) = P(a)P(c|a) = (.6)(.7) = .42$. The coherence interval in this case of MP is then from .42 to .72, and our judgement that $P(c) = .6$ is coherent. Recall the singularity principle from Section 3.4 and note that people will still be coherent, at the minimum of the interval, even if singularity causes them to focus on $P(c|a)$ and in effect judge that $P(c|not\text{-}a) = 0$. This principle does not necessarily make people incoherent.

But a judgement that $P(c) = .95$ would be incoherent and a kind of overconfidence, and one that $P(c) = .25$ would be incoherent and a kind of underconfidence. These judgements could also be called a type of 'belief bias' resulting from too much belief in c, or too little belief in c, than MP justifies. There is also a coherence interval for AC, inferring a from *if a then c* and c, and other conditional inferences. Evans at al. (2015) found that people stay within these coherence intervals at an above chance rate, just as they conform to p-validity above chance (Section 3.2), and they do even better by both measures when the premises and conclusions are presented together for explicit inferences and not judged separately.

Edgington (1995) argued strongly for the Equation, but she suggested that it might be disconfirmed for pragmatically problematic conditionals, as she presupposed, like the following:

(5.3) If Napoleon is dead (n), Oxford is in England (o).

She remarked that many people might judge (5.3) as ' . . . not acceptable, or even, false'. The Equation/conditional probability hypothesis implies that (5.3) will be assessed as highly probable and not definitely false, since $P(o|n)$ is high. In general, $P(q|p)$ is high when $P(q)$ is high and p and q are independent. Pragmatically unacceptable conditionals like (5.3) are sometimes called 'missing-link' conditionals, but this term can be misleading, as there are pragmatically acceptable conditionals with 'missing-links' in some sense, for example, (3.3) above, 'If Arthur is not in Edinburgh, then he is in Scotland'. In sharp contrast, conditionals like (5.3) are not pragmatically all right, and we will call them *Walrus conditionals* (Cruz & Over, 2024; Over, 2023b). In Lewis Carroll's nonsense poem, 'The Walrus and the carpenter', the Walrus says, ' . . . the time has come to talk of many things: of shoes, and ships, and sealing-wax, of cabbages, and kings'. The Walrus's 'conversation' is a pragmatically bizarre jumble, and a Walrus conditional is similar. Its antecedent and consequent do not have a pragmatic or semantic relation to each other in a given context.

Skovgaard-Olsen et al. (2016) confirmed Edgington's suggestion about what we are calling Walrus conditionals. They tested the conditional probability hypothesis, that $P(if\ p\ then\ q) = P(q|p)$, and found that participants in an experiment did judge $P(if\ p\ then\ q)$ to be lower than $P(q|p)$ for Walrus conditionals (see Over & Cruz, 2023, on Skovgaard-Olsen et al.'s findings about non-Walrus conditionals). In reply, Cruz et al. (2016) hypothesised that the problem with Walrus conditionals is that they do not contain a common topic of discourse, and they provided experimental support for this hypothesis (as do Bourlier et al., 2023). Lassiter (2023) develops the concept of *pragmatic discourse coherence*. This is much wider than *logical* coherence, which is consistency with probability theory. He explains why (to use our terms) Walrus 'conversations' and Walrus conditionals do not have pragmatic discourse coherence, unless a special context is given for them.

It was a significant step forward for Skovgaard-Olsen et al. to investigate Walrus conditionals and establish their result about them, but compare these three conditionals:

(5.4) If Mark presses the power button on his TV, then the TV will be turned on.

(5.5) If Mark is wearing socks (w), then his TV will be working (v).

(5.6) If Mark presses the power button on his TV, then the screen will remain blank.

Conditionals like (5.4) are *dependence conditionals*: their antecedents increase the probability of their consequents. Conditionals like (5.5) and (5.6) could be vaguely said to have missing causal or other 'links' and can be more precisely termed *independence conditionals* (Cruz & Over, 2023). In these conditionals, the consequent is independent of the antecedent, for example, $P(v|w) = P(v|not\text{-}w)$. But there is a big difference between (5.5) and (5.6). For (5.5) does not have pragmatic discourse coherence, and that makes it a Walrus conditional. Skovgaard-Olsen et al. compared conditionals like (5.4) and (5.5) with each other, finding that only probability judgements about the dependence conditional (5.4) complied with the conditional probability hypothesis. But going from (5.4) to (5.5), they changed a pragmatically acceptable dependence conditional into a pragmatically unacceptable independence conditional, that is, a Walrus conditional (Cruz & Over, 2024; Over, 2023b). This confound could be avoided in the future by asking for probability judgements about conditionals like (5.4) and (5.6), which are both pragmatically acceptable. In (5.6), we have an example of a non-Walrus independence conditional that could pragmatically convey useful information about Mark's TV.

There is a debate about the significance of experiments on 'missing-link' or Walrus conditionals. There is an *inferentialist* view that a 'standard' conditional *if p then q* is true if and only if there is a non-redundant deductive, or sufficiently strong inductive, abductive, or other non-deductive, relation between p and q (Douven et al., 2023; van Rooij et al., 2023). This semantic proposal implies that the conditional probability hypothesis fails for Walrus conditionals because these conditionals are supposedly not true. On the other side of the debate, theorists argue for Edgington's original presupposition that pragmatics can fully explain the problem with Walrus conditionals (Bourlier et al., 2023; Cruz & Over, 2023, 2024; Lassiter, 2023; Over & Cruz, 2023). There is experimental evidence that people classify Walrus conditionals *if p then q* as 'true' when p and q are true (see Skovgaard-Olsen et al., 2017, on 'irrelevance' cases), and also strong support for the conditional probability hypothesis in experiments where the materials are pragmatically acceptable (see Sections 2.6 and 5.1 and additionally Kleiter et al., 2018, Oberauer et al., 2007, Pfeifer, 2023, Singmann et al., 2014, and Wang et al., 2022).

The relation $P(q|p) > P(q|not\text{-}p)$ holds for dependence conditionals. This is the formal equivalent of stating that p raises the probability of q. But there are grounds for concluding that this relation is neither necessary nor sufficient for pragmatic acceptability. The de Finetti (1937/1964) *normal form* for *if p then q* is *if p then (p & q)*. Note that, although $P(q|p)$ and $P((p \ \& \ q)|p)$ are necessarily equal, *if p then (p & q)* can be dependence conditional when *if p then q* is an independence conditional. Consider the normal form of (5.5), that is, *if w then (w & v)*. Now $P(v|w) = P(v|not\text{-}w) = P((w \ \& \ v)|w) = P(v)$, and yet we have $P((w \ \& \ v)|w) > P((w \ \& \ v)|not\text{-}w)$ when $P(v)$ is not 0. Therefore, 'If Mark is wearing socks, then he is wearing socks and his TV will be working' is a dependence conditional, but that is intuitively not sufficient to make it more pragmatically acceptable than 'If Mark is wearing socks, then his TV will be working'.

As we have already illustrated with (3.3) and (5.6), there are pragmatically acceptable conditionals which are independence and not dependence conditionals. For another example, doctors could say to parents whose children are known not to have autism:

(5.7) If your children are vaccinated, they will not get autism.

The pragmatic implication of (5.7) is that whether children will get autism is independent of whether they have vaccinations. Knowing about independence, and conveying information about it using conditionals, is of great utility in human reasoning and decision-making (Cruz & Over, 2023; Over, 2023b). It is to the advantage of suppositional theories that they give unified accounts of dependence and independence conditionals.

5.3 Dynamic Reasoning and Counterfactuals

Experiments have strongly supported the conditional probability hypothesis, $P(if\ p\ then\ q) = P(q|p)$ for conditionals with pragmatic discourse coherence, and subjective conditional probability theory can guide us in our static and dynamic conditional reasoning. There are the logical coherence intervals we have described for reasoning in a static state, when our degrees of belief do not change over time, and on top of these, we have the Bayesian notions of strict and Jeffrey conditionalisation for dynamic reasoning when our beliefs are updated over time (Section 3.4; Oaksford & Chater, 2020).

We can illustrate some more points about dynamic reasoning using the example of an investigation of a crime. Suppose that a precious jewel has apparently been stolen at a country house, and the police have high confidence that:

(5.8) The butler stole the jewel (b) or the cook did (k).

On this basis, they can also infer with some confidence that:

(5.9) If the butler did not steal the jewel, the cook did.

Let us use P_1 for the police's probability judgements early in their investigations of this case, and P_2 for their later probability judgements. Notice immediately that, assuming (5.9) is a suppositional conditional, the inference from (5.8) to (5.9) is not p-valid and will only be probabilistically strong in some contexts. (5.8) will be highly probable when it is inferred simply from strong evidence that the butler stole the jewel, making $P_1(b)$ high, but then (5.9) can have a very low probability, with $P_1(k|not\text{-}b)$ at or near 0 in this context (Cruz et al., 2015; Gilio & Over, 2012).

However, let us suppose that the police have general grounds for judging that the probability of (5.8) is relatively high. For example, the butler and cook are the only suspects without alibis. The police can then have relatively high confidence in (5.9). Let us also say $P_1(b) = P_1(k) = .5$, and $P_1(k|not\text{-}b) = .9$. After later finding definite evidence that the butler did not steal the jewel, $P_2(not\text{-}b) = 1$ the police could use Bayesian strict conditionalisation (Section 3.4) to infer $P_2(k) = P_1(k|not\text{-}b) = .9$, provided that *invariance* in the conditional probabilities holds, $P_2(k|not\text{-}b) = P_1(k|not\text{-}b)$. Invariance can fail when new information is acquired in the change from P_1 to P_2, as would happen if the police were to discover that the jewel was not stolen, but only misplaced. In that case, $P_2(k)$ and $P_2(k|not\text{-}b)$ would both be 0.

Suppose, however, that the police become more and more convinced in dynamic reasoning that the butler stole the jewel. At some point in this process, they might start to use *counterfactual* conditionals, beginning with 'If the butler had not stolen the jewel ...', but they could reject as improbable:

(5.10) If the butler had not stolen the jewel, then the cook would have.

Using the Ramsey test (Section 5.1), the police could reason that the cook would not be turned into a criminal supposing something intervened to prevent the butler from stealing the jewel (see Pearl, 2013, on Ramsey's 'idea', and Kaufmann, 2023, for a temporal analysis of counterfactuals). If they got still more evidence and started to go backwards, losing their confidence that the butler is the culprit, their counterfactual thought (5.10) could return to the indicative (5.9) and their previously high confidence in that. In recent years, psychologists of reasoning have used Bayesian networks (Pearl, 2000) to represent people's conditional reasoning about causes (Oaksford & Chater, 2020), but much more research is needed on how people move in their reasoning from indicative conditionals to counterfactuals and, sometimes, back again (Over & Cruz, 2023).

There is much research in psychology on counterfactuals and the emotions, especially regret (see Corbett et al., 2023, on how the two are linked in human beings even at a young age). Recall yet again the cryptocurrency scheme and suppose it does turn out to be a scam. We could express regret in this way:

(5.11) If we had not invested in that scheme, we would not look like fools.

But assume our decision about the scheme was a long time ago, and we have numerous investments, making it hard to remember the details. When we consult our accountants, they tell us that we did not in fact make that investment, and we use (5.11) as the major premise of MP to infer that we do not look like fools. Then our regret vanishes. People do conform to MP when the major premise is a counterfactual (see Thompson & Byrne, 2002, and Over & Cruz, 2023, for comment). But psychologists do not have an account of how, or why, logical reasoning with counterfactuals is so closely tied to people's emotions, and philosophers have so far paid no attention to this link in their theories of counterfactuals.

5.4 Conclusion

The compliance of humans with the Equation or conditional probability hypothesis, $P(if\ p\ then\ q) = P(q|p)$, has been strongly confirmed in psychological experiments for pragmatically acceptable conditionals. This provides empirical support for suppositional theories of conditionals in which *if p then q* can be read as *q supposing p*, and *P(if p then q) = P(q|p)*. Ramsey and de Finetti laid the theoretical foundations for these theories, which cover both dependence and independence conditionals and can be extended to dynamic reasoning and belief updating. There is an above chance tendency for people to reason within the logical coherence intervals of suppositional conditionals, and also comply with p-validity, especially in their explicit conditional reasoning, but whether this tendency makes them rational is a question for Section 7.

6 Dual Processes in Reasoning

Dual-process theories have played – and continue to play – a significant role in the psychology of reasoning. As we shall see, these accounts form part of a family of theories whose origins predate modern cognitive psychology. They are independent of the new paradigm, which reflects a shift in thinking about *how* people reason and the relevant normative standards to apply. Dual-process theory is more concerned with the question of *when* people apply explicit reasoning to produce their answers, as opposed to faster and lower effort intuitive processes. In this section, we will briefly review the dual-process framework and more specifically the history of dual-process theories in the psychology of reasoning.

A distinction between two kinds of thinking, one slow and reflective and the other fast and intuitive has been around for hundreds of years in philosophical writing and has featured heavily in 'modern' cognitive and social psychology (Frankish & Evans, 2009). By modern, we mean roughly post-1960, which is about the date of the cognitive revolution in psychology, in which information processing models of the mind displaced the behaviourism that had been dominant for the previous fifty years. The idea of nonconscious and conscious thinking has figured in many accounts. Important origins in modern psychology include work on implicit learning by Reber, which originally predated the cognitive revolution (see Reber, 1993, for an overview of this research programme). While the cognitive revolution largely caused a switch of focus from implicit to explicit memory systems (Frankish & Evans, 2009), some authors such as Reber and others continued to emphasise the contrast between the two, and the fact that some kinds of knowledge can be acquired implicitly without any awareness of a learning process (see Cleeremans, 2015; Cleeremans & Kuvaldina, 2019 for overviews of this field of work).

A number of the dichotomies associated with broad dual-process accounts are shown in Table 4, but these are by no means exhaustive. We have used the labels Type 1 and Type 2 here. The terms System 1 and System 2, introduced by Stanovich (1999) became popular and are still used by some authors (e.g., Kahneman, 2011),

Table 4 Dichotomies and features that have been associated with dual processes in thinking by various authors

Type 1	Type 2
Intuitive	Reflective
Non-conscious	Conscious
Fast	Slow
Automatic	Controlled
Associative	Rule based
Implicit knowledge	Explicit knowledge
Contextualised	Abstract
High capacity	Low capacity
Independent of general intelligence	Correlated with general intelligence
Independent of working memory	Imposes load on working memory

but the notion of dual systems is problematic. A number of authors have suggested that the two systems could have roots in evolutionary distinct systems, System 1 being associated with more animal-like cognition and System 2 more distinctively human (e.g., Epstein, 1994; Evans & Over, 1996; Reber, 1993; Stanovich, 2004), but this seems to us now to be an unhelpful way to use the word 'system'. We now prefer to describe such approaches as *two minds* theories, a concept explored in detail by Evans (2010). System 1 cannot be a single system as there are multiple kinds of Type 1 process (Evans & Stanovich, 2013), and there are also arguments for multiple Type 2 systems (Evans, 2019). Hence, the Type 1 and 2 terminology seems to be the clearest.

Theories of dual processes, systems, and minds raise a very large and complex set of questions which we cannot possibly deal with in this short section. We will focus here primality on dual-process accounts within the psychology of reasoning. First, however, we draw attention to the distinction between unconscious and *precon-scious* processes. There are very many wholly unconscious inferential processes in the brain, such as those used for visual perception and language comprehension, which are not part of our story here. Type 1 processes (see Table 4) are better thought of as preconscious in that they post some final product into consciousness (or working memory), typically a putative intuitive judgement accompanied by a feeling of confidence (Thompson et al., 2011). Type 2 processes, in contrast, post intermediate products into working memory so that we have some conscious sense of the process of reasoning. It is the required use of a capacity-limited singular working memory system (Baddeley, 2007, 2020) that makes Type 2 processes relatively slow. Some theorists (e.g., Engle, 2002) also equate working memory with *controlled attention*, linking with the automatic-controlled dichotomy, popular in dual-process writing.

6.1 Matching and Belief Biases: Origins of Modern Dual-Process Theories

Peter Wason is often regarded as the founder of the modern psychology of reasoning (Manktelow, 2021), and the second author was fortunate enough to have had him as his PhD supervisor. Among other things, Wason was an inventor of reasoning problems which have led to hundreds of published studies in the literature. We have already met his 2–4–6 task (Wason, 1960) in Section 4.1. His most famous problem, however, is the four-card selection task, usually known just as the selection task, first introduced to an unsuspecting audience in an early book chapter (Wason, 1966). It has since become the single most cited and investigated task in the whole psychology of reasoning (Evans, 2022). The original problem used abstract materials, and a typical example is shown in Figure 2. In essence, people are asked to test the truth of a conditional statement about cards which have a letter on one side and a number on the other. In the example shown, the claim is that if there is an A one side then there is a 3 on the other. In Wason's original experiment four actual cards were used with a human experimenter sitting across at a table, but in most later experiments,

There are four cards lying on a table. Each has a capital letter on one side and a single digit number on the other side. The exposed sides are shown below:

The rule shown below applies to these four cards and may be true or false:

If there is an A on one side of the card, then there is a 3 on the other side of the card

Your task is to decide those cards, and only those cards, that need to be turned over in order to discover whether the rule is true or false.

Figure 2 Standard abstract version of the Wason selection task

a diagram similar to that in Figure 2 is shown on a computer screen and cards can be selected by pointing and clicking with a mouse. The important feature is that each card has a visible facing side and a hidden side. All we know for sure is that a letter has a number hidden on the back and vice versa. The visible values are A, D, 3 and 7.

The task is not purely deductive as it involves hypothesis testing, but it does test whether people understand that the statement could be disproved by finding a card which has an A on one side, but a number other than a 3 on the other. Logically, they could only discover this if the A card was turned over to display some other number, or if the 7 card (an example of a number which is not a 3) turned out to have an A on the back. Given that the task is stated to be only about the four displayed cards, Wason and most (but not all) later researchers consider the correct choice to be the A and the 7. The claim will be true for these four cards unless proven false, and only turning the A and the 7 could do that. Many studies have shown that participants, typically but not always undergraduate students, make this choice only about 10 per cent of the time. As Wason discovered, most people select either the A card alone, or the A and the 3. Choosing 3 could not disprove the statement, of course which makes no claim that an A must be on the back of a 3. The A could, but so could the 7, so both need to be chosen to comply with the instructions. So elusive is the correct solution that Wason (1966) claimed that even professors of logic were known to get it wrong!

Wason's original explanation of the problem was a verification bias, better known now as confirmation bias. (He maintained the view that he had demonstrated such a bias with his 2–4–6 problem, a claim now seen as highly dubious, as discussed in Section 4.) He believed that people were trying to prove the statement true rather than false, and hence looking for the confirming case of A and 3. In the original paper he also proposed that people have a 'defective truth table' for the conditional (see Section 5), in which the statement was seen as irrelevant to letters other than A. This explains why the D card is hardly ever selected, but not why people often choose the 3 card, unless they take the statement as a biconditional. The alternative account was *matching bias*. That is, people chose A and 3 simply because they matched the content of the conditional statement. In order to demonstrate this, negations have to be introduced into the conditional. For example, suppose the problem is the same as shown in Figure 2 except that the conditional statement is 'If there is an A on one side of the card, then there is not a 3 on the other side of the card'.

If cards are chosen to verify, then the participants should select the A and 7 (not the 3) cards, but if they are matching, they will continue to choose A and 3, even though this is now the logically correct choice, as it can uncover a falsifying case. The latter is what participants actually do, as originally demonstrated by Evans and Lynch (1973) and replicated many times since. Good Popperian as he was, Wason immediately accepted that his verification bias account must be wrong, he but was nevertheless puzzled by the finding. The main reason for his curiosity was that he had recently shown that when asked to provide a short verbal justification for their card choices, people appeared to show understanding of the logic (Goodwin & Wason, 1972). That is, they described their choices as verifying or falsifying the statement, consistent with their card selections. As a result, Wason and Evans (1975) ran an experiment combining the two methods. They used both the affirmative and negative conditional forms, but also asked participants to provide a short, written justification for each card choice. Participants performed both tasks, half affirmative followed by negative and half vice versa. The results of this simple and single experiment launched the dual-process theory in the psychology of reasoning. (Their findings were never contested and were eventually replicated in all essential details by Lucas and Ball, 2005.)

First, Wason and Evans replicated the matching bias account. Participants' predominant choices were the equivalent of A and 3 on both versions of the task (of course, actual lexical content was varied randomly). However, they also replicated Goodwin and Wason, in that explanations offered were always logically consistent with the card choices made. This meant that on the negative tasks, people generally showed 'insight', saying that they were choosing A and 3 in order to prove the statement false, but on the usual affirmative versions they continued to justify their choices as seeking a confirming combination of A and 3. This applied equally to those receiving the negative version first. So how could a negative stimulate 'insight' which was then immediately lost when the negative was removed?

The explanation offered by Wason and Evans was that participants' card choices were influenced by an unconscious Type 1 process (they actually used the now modern terms Type 1 and 2) but that the verbal justifications were generated by a second, separate process of Type 2 reasoning. In effect, they were *rationalisations*. In a second study, (Evans & Wason, 1976) showed that participants would provide a rationalisation for any of several common patterns of card choices that were implied to be the correct choice by the experimenters, even though only one was. They gave a justification of verification and/or falsification with high confidence, regardless of the 'solution' being justified. Hence, the original form of the dual-process theory of reasoning was that of preconscious intuition followed by conscious rationalisation. This is important, because later versions mutated into a different account in which Type 1 and Type 2 processes compete for control of the response, with the suggestion that Type 2 reasoning was required for correct logical reasoning. Evans, (2019) has discussed in detail the origin and nature of these two forms of dual-process theory and their potential for reconciliation. The original rationalisation form of the theory is still preferred by contemporary authors who believe that reasoning evolved for the purpose of argumentation rather than problem-solving (Mercier & Sperber, 2011, 2017).

The second form, which we might call the *conflict theory*, was stimulated by the study of belief bias in syllogistic reasoning already described (Sections 2.3 and 2.4; Evans et al., 1983). In view of our discussion of the new paradigm, the reader may wonder if it is still right to refer to this effect as a cognitive 'bias'. It is now held to be permissible, and even obligatory, for people to take account of their prior beliefs in reasoning, as long as this is consistent with Bayesian principles (Section 3). But the term 'belief bias' persists in the contemporary literature and strictly speaking it is a bias when observed in experiments with instructions requiring participants to disregard prior belief. It also turns out that the ability to comply with such instructions – or not – is a key factor in dual-process accounts. These are the main reasons 'belief bias' continues to be used in some contemporary studies. In deference to the new paradigm, however, we will refer to the *belief effect* in this section, avoiding the term 'bias'.

The reader may recall that in the study of Evans et al. (1983) participants were influenced by both the logical validity of the conclusions offered and their prior believability. Also, this belief effect was stronger for invalid than valid arguments. One account, favoured by the original authors as well as later in a mental model theory (Oakhill et al., 1989), is known as *selective scrutiny*. That is, participants are more motivated to examine the logical basis for unbelievable conclusions, or to seek counterexample mental models which demonstrate their invalidity. This means that reasoning is motivated by *disbelief* in line with cognitive miser principle (Stanovich, 2018). Why bother challenging the evidence for an assertion you already believe? This explains why the belief effect is stronger for invalid arguments, but not why it is still significantly present for valid arguments. Nevertheless, the belief effect studies stimulated the view that belief-based intuitions may *compete* with logical reasoning, a conclusion supported by some experimental findings. For example, the belief effect is stronger and logical accuracy weaker when very short time limits are given (Evans & Curtis-Holmes, 2005), presumably because there is insufficient time for Type 2 reasoning.

These positions have led to some detailed debate and investigation in the recent psychological literature (see Evans et al., 2022, pp. 161–164). We do not have space to review these studies here but in essence there is a distinction being drawn between a Type 1 belief effect (across the board tendency towards believable conclusions) and a Type 2 belief effect, which is motivated reasoning selectively applied when conclusions are unbelievable. An important recent contribution has been the idea that on reasoning and judgement tasks, a quick intuitive answer comes to mind with a degree of confidence known as feeling of rightness (FOR) (Thompson et al., 2011). The evidence shows that people are more likely to rethink or change an intuitive answer if it has low FOR, which is a kind of selective scrutiny. Correspondingly, participants have been shown to have higher FOR for believable than unbelievable conclusions (Thompson et al., 2011) and also for matching than mismatching cards on the selection task (Thompson et al., 2013). There has also been a good deal of interest in the Cognitive Reflection Test (Frederick, 2005; Toplak et al., 2011), a set of simple looking problems with intuitively compelling answers that are actually wrong. Such tasks are often failed by those of high intelligence who do not look beyond intuition. Intuitive confidence and selective processing accord with the 'cognitive miser' hypothesis, which postulates that in a world of massive information overload we evolved to use our central cognitive resources as selectively as possible (Stanovich, 2018). Intuitive confidence can, however, easily be misplaced in the modern world.

6.2 Dual Processes and Individual Differences

Individual differences in cognitive ability have been studied by psychologists for over a century, with Spearman (1904) presenting the first theory of general intelligence – also known as just *g* – which led to a major field of study and the later invention of IQ testing. For a history, and review of recent research on intelligence see Deary (2020). In essence, there is strong evidence that there is indeed a general factor of intelligence, largely hereditary, that correlates with academic attainment and all manner of cognitive tasks, especially those involving reasoning and calculation.

Dual-process theory is mostly studied by experimental means. It is widely accepted that Type 2 processing (or explicit reasoning) requires use of short-term and capacity-limited working memory store (Evans & Stanovich, 2013). Working memory has been subject to an enormous number of studies in the memory literature, largely separated from the study of reasoning and decision making (see Baddeley, 2007, 2020, for the history of this research programme). However, cognitive psychologists studying reasoning are well aware of this work and its methods. One can try to inhibit Type 2 reasoning, for example, by asking people to reason with concurrent working memory loads, or by instruction to respond immediately without thought. However, one can also apply a psychometric approach, arguing that tasks that require Type 2 reasoning should be correlated with individual differences in general intelligence. This is the basis of a long-standing research programme by Keith Stanovich and Ricard West from the 1990s onwards (Stanovich, 1999, 2011; Stanovich & West, 2000). We should also note that there have now been many studies of individual differences in measured working-memory capacity (WMC), which also correlated with performance on a huge range of cognitive tasks (see Baddeley, 2007). These measures are themselves highly correlated with general intelligence, although the size of the correlation is disputed. At the very least, however, we can say that those high in general intelligence are likely to have higher working memory capacity and are therefore also likely to be better at Type 2 reasoning.

Stanovich and West have studied a large range of reasoning and decision tasks drawn from cognitive and social psychology usually using SAT scores as a surrogate for general intelligence (SAT is, in psychometric speak, highly g-loaded). Among many other similar findings, they have shown that performance on the abstract Wason selection task is related to general intelligence (Stanovich & West, 1998) as in the ability to resist the influence of belief in syllogistic reasoning (Stanovich et al., 1999). In a recent huge scale and comprehensive study, they showed that general intelligence is implicated in the vast majority of known cognitive tasks on which well-established errors and cognitive biases are demonstrated (Stanovich et al., 2016). However, there is one important exception: *myside bias*. This is the tendency to value and propose only arguments which accord with one's core values and worldview. Myside bias is equally marked in those of higher intelligence, education level and rational thinking style. This exceptionality is so important that Stanovich has recently written a whole book about myside thinking (Stanovich, 2021). We discuss myside bias in Section 7.

From the beginning, Stanovich and West have argued that, although general intelligence facilitates Type 2 reasoning and the avoidance of cognitive biases, it is not the only basis for rational thinking. Indeed, Stanovich has written another book on what he sees as the fallacy that measured intelligence equates with rationality (Stanovich, 2009). In all of their studies, they show that when the variance due to intelligence is removed, there remains a second important predictor, which is self-reported rational thinking style. In essence, it is not enough to have a high IQ to be smart, you must also have the disposition and motivation to apply Type 2 reasoning to the problem in hand. People high in rational thinking style do not rely on intuition when solving novel or difficult problems but check their potential solutions out with explicit reasoning. It is well known that when problems solicit particularly plausible but incorrect solutions, even those of high intelligence will often fail to solve them. We will return to Stanovich's writing about rationality in Section 7.

6.3 Debate and Controversy about Dual-Process Theory

In hindsight, both Keith Stanovich and Jonathan Evans realised that they inadvertently contributed to the creation of myth in dual-process theory, which we term the *normative fallacy*. The fallacy is that Type 1 processes are responsible for cognitive biases and errors and Type 2 processes generate normatively correct answers. In the most extreme application of the fallacy, some authors write as though one could diagnose the type of processing underlying a judgement or inference from the normative accuracy of the answer given.

The normative fallacy must be wrong for a number of reasons. Type 1 processes certainly can lead to cognitive biases, especially with abstract and novel laboratory tasks such as the Cognitive Reflection Test. Moreover, our subjective feelings of confidence are far from reliable and can be attached to wrong as well as right answers (Thompson et al., 2011). However, experts with experience and others can develop accurate intuitions which often allow them to respond rapidly and appropriately to real world situations, as a number of authors have argued (Gigerenzer, 2007; Gladwell, 2005; Klein, 1998). Much of this helpful intuition takes the form of rapid pattern recognition. The evidence for such accurate intuitions is beyond dispute, so Type 1 intuitive processes alone cannot be identified with cognitive biases.

Equally, Type 2 processing does not and cannot guarantee correct responding (see Elqayam & Evans, 2011, and Section 7). Type 2 reasoning can fail for a number of reasons. People may have insufficient cognitive capacity for the problem or lack relevant knowledge or 'mindware'. They may also try to simplify their reasoning by focusing on only a single possibility, when more are relevant, as described by the singularity principle (Section 3.4) and consistent with the cognitive miser hypothesis (Stanovich, 2018). All of these things have been pointed out repeatedly by both Evans and Stanovich (e.g., Evans, 2007b; Stanovich, 2011). So how did these authors contribute to the fallacy? The answer is by focussing much dual-process research on particular laboratory tasks that are novel, abstract, and difficult, and to which real world experience is hard to apply. Deductive reasoning can be difficult, for example, and prior knowledge is biasing by definition in the old, traditional paradigm (see Section 2). Without logical training, people will frequently commit fallacies, and without high general intelligence, they will find it hard to follow instructions to assume premises and disregard their prior beliefs (see Section 2). These laboratory tasks are selected for dual-process research precisely because Type 2 reasoning is necessary (but not sufficient) for their solution, so that we can make it more or less easy to apply, for example by the use of time limits, instructional sets or working memory loads.

Misunderstanding of dual-process theory goes much deeper than the normative fallacy, however. There has been a tendency for critics to assume that the typical correlated features of the two types of processing shown in Table 4 are all necessary and defining features. Such a position is easily refutable, of course, but has been assumed by a number of leading critics (e.g., Keren & Schul, 2009; Kruglanski & Gigerenzer, 2011). However, to our knowledge, no particular dual-process theorist has proposed this perfect alignment of attributes. This is part of what Evans and Stanovich (2013) call the 'received' version of dual-process theory, a generic and simplified version which is attacked by critics while being proposed by no author in particular. Other criticisms considered by Evans and Stanovich include vague and multiple definitions, the idea that processing varies on a continuum rather than a dichotomy (Kruglanski & Gigerenzer, 2011; Osman, 2004), and a lack of convincing empirical evidence. Evans and Stanovich offer rebuttals of all these arguments and particularly the last.

An important distinction between dual-process theories lies in whether they propose a parallel or serial architecture. The two main types are known as *parallel-competitive* and *default-interventionist* (Evans, 2007b). In the parallel form (Sloman, 1996; Smith & DeCoster, 1999), what they term 'rule-based' (Type 2) and 'associative' (Type 1) processes proceed in a parallel and the individual may become aware of a conflict between the two. More commonly advanced, however, is the default-interventionist form, favoured by Evans and Stanovich and other leading theorists (e.g., Kahneman, 2011). In this version, rapid Type 1 processes generate a default intuitive response which may or may not be overridden by subsequent, slower Type 2 reasoning. The tendency to override can be influenced by motivation provided by either the reasoner (rational thinking style) or the intuition itself (feeling of rightness). Intervention which successfully avoids a cognitive bias also depends upon having sufficient time and cognitive resources available and on the possession of prior relevant knowledge or 'mindware' (Stanovich, 2011, 2018). Evans (2019) has proposed that Type 1 intuitions are always scrutinised to some extent by Type 2 processes, but the latter often serve only to rationalise the intuition. The scrutiny can, however, lead to a rethink in which Type 2 reasoning substitutes an alternative response. The complexity of these accounts exposes the simplistic nature of the normative fallacy.

In recent years, there have been questions for standard dual-processing accounts raised by some reasoning researchers, who have suggested that people might have *logical intuitions* (De Neys, 2012, 2022). On a variety of problems, people have been shown to detect the normatively correct answer very rapidly, as evidenced by a variety of cognitive and neuroscientific measures. It has also been claimed that the logic of a reasoning problem can interfere with judgements to decide the believability of a conclusion (Handley et al., 2011), in a reversal of the evidence normally claimed to show that 'belief bias' research supports dual-process theory. There are also papers showing that people of higher intelligence may have more accurate intuitions, which cannot be attributed to better Type 2 reasoning ability (Thompson et al., 2018).

In commenting on these studies (Evans, 2018, 2019) has pointed to the very simple nature of the tasks used in these experiments, in which the normative response could easily be produced rapidly. For example, Handley et al.'s findings showed that it was more difficult to judge a conclusion unbelievable when it was derived by a Modus Ponens inference. But MP is arguably provided automatically by the language module (Braine & O'Brien, 1991). To infer that a correct answer necessarily results from Type 2 reasoning is, of course, the normative fallacy. A recent paper by Ghasemi et al. (2022) confirms this interpretation of the studies (see also Ghasemi et al., 2023). They showed that intuitive inferences can be rapidly generated from structural features (as well as beliefs), but that such inferences may or may not be logically accurate. For example, the conclusion of AC has 'pseudovalidity' such that it will interfere with conflicting belief judgements, in just the same way as occurs for the actually valid MP inference. Intuitions flow from structure as well as beliefs, but of course we already knew that from examples such as atmosphere effects in syllogistic reasoning (Section 2.2) and matching bias on the selection task.

In conclusion, we agree with critics that the 'received' version of dual-process theory is wrong. There is no Type 2 process which is invariably slow and normatively correct, for example. Type 1 intuitions need not be belief based and can be accurate. However, neither we nor other authors have proposed such a theory. The dual-process theory of reasoning has evolved into a much more nuanced and complex account as a mass of evidence has been collected. Simple generalisations about the two types of processing are not sustainable, and some would argue that this makes it hard to falsify the theory. However, it is important to understand the framework which has motivated so much research over the past forty years or so. Type 2 reasoning corresponds to the kinds of reasoning normally discussed in philosophy, but psychologists have shown that this reasoning is also influenced by rapid preconscious processes, and that a large number of factors can affect its conclusions, including those related to the presentation of the reasoning problem and its context, and the individual nature of the person doing the reasoning.

7 Rationality and Reasoning

Experimental studies of reasoning, as well as of judgement and decision-making (JDM, not generally covered in this Element), have evoked a 'great rationality debate' (Stanovich, 2011). This debate in psychology was started by a philosopher, L. Jonathan Cohen (1981), and many philosophers and psychologists have contributed to it. Psychologists of reasoning and JDM cannot escape discussion of rationality owing to their common use of normative theories to assess error and bias. We saw in Section 2 that the deductive paradigm, based on classical logic, was eventually challenged and modified by the new paradigm, which we have discussed at length in this Element. Essentially, the inability of participants to comply with classical reasoning from assumptions, and with the material conditional analysis of the natural language conditional, forced psychologists either to declare people inherently irrational, or else to question the normative accounts that judged them to be in error. As we have shown, most took the latter path. In this section, we will explore several aspects of rationality and human reasoning. But we will begin with a brief historical review of the rationality debate as it developed.

7.1 The Great Rationality Debate

Evans (2021) has recently reviewed the history of the rationality debate in detail, and we will give only a brief summary here. As we have already shown, Peter Wason was publishing studies of reasoning from the 1960s onwards, leading to a widely read and influential book summarising much of this work and its conclusions (Wason & Johnson-Laird, 1972). Wason's claims of confirmation bias (later disputed) and other evidence of logical error and bias led him directly to conclusions of irrationality, writing later, 'It could be argued that irrationality rather than rationality is the norm. People all too readily succumb to logical fallacies' (Wason, 1983). From the early 1970s onwards, the revolutionary research of Daniel Kahneman and Amos Tversky had massive influence on the study of judgement and decision making. JDM researchers in the 1960s thought that human decision-making was fairly rational, provided that probabilities were allowed to be subjective, but Kahneman and Tversky demonstrated a whole range of cognitive biases in a series of highly influential articles.

Their general thesis was that people judge probabilities by applying heuristics such as those based on *representativeness* (Section 5.3) and *availability* (Tversky & Kahneman, 1974). Although often useful, these heuristics could lead to biases. For example, the availability heuristic is used when we judge frequency by the ease with which examples can be brought to mind. Thus, doctors when confronted with a patient's symptoms might recall similar cases in their experience and use these to determine a probable diagnosis. However, as Kahneman and Tversky demonstrated, this heuristic can often lead to biases due to how our memories work. If shown a list of names that includes famous as well as unknown people, for example, participants will overestimate the frequency of the famous ones as they are easier to recall. Doctors could also be biased if they recalled a patient with similar symptoms but an unusual diagnosis who was especially memorable, say, as a close family friend. Following the early papers of Kahneman and Tversky, a very large field of research built up demonstrating many judgemental biases both in the laboratory and in real world settings (Gilovich et al., 2002; Kahneman et al., 1982).

Kahneman and Tversky were more cautious than Wason about attributing irrationality to their participants, but many of their followers were less restrained. Cohen (1981) read widely in the psychology of reasoning and JDM and came to the conclusion that psychologists were overstating their case. In fact, he claimed that irrationality *could never* be demonstrated by such experiments, a position later dubbed *Panglossian* (Stanovich, 2011). As the second author has observed (e.g., Evans, 2021) there were three main arguments in Cohen's paper which Evans terms:

1. The normative system problem
2. The interpretation problem
3. The external validity problem

The *normative system problem* is that psychologists were wont to adopt standard normative theories, such as classical logic, whereas philosophers and others had provided many alternative normative accounts of reasoning and decision-making. One should not therefore simply judge people right or wrong by uncritically presupposing some norm. Of course, Cohen was right about this and the problem of alternative norms for psychological research was discussed in detail more recently by Elqayam and Evans (2011). We have already shown in this Element how the new paradigm psychology of reasoning emerged due to dissatisfaction with classical logic as a normative account of deduction. We should also note the claim of Stanovich (e.g., 2011) that it is compliance with classical norms of logic that generally correlates with intelligence and rationality thinking measures, while also recalling that there is considerable overlap in the norms of classical logic and probability logic. For example, as we have pointed out above, in Section 2.4, MP and MT are both valid in classical logic and p-valid (Section 3.2) in probability logic, and AC and DA are both invalid in classical logic and p-invalid in probability logic.

The *interpretation problem* is that the participants may not understand the problem in the way in which the experimenter intended. Take as an example, the conjunction fallacy described in Sections 3.2 and 4.3 (Tversky & Kahneman, 1983). Given a stereotype suggesting that Linda is a radical young woman, people may judge that 'Linda is a feminist and a bank teller' to be more probable than 'Linda is a bank teller'. This judgement might seem to be logically incoherent and a fallacy, but when the two sentences are included in the same list, it is possible that participants take the second to mean implicitly 'Linda is a bank teller *who is not a feminist*', in which case there is no fallacy. The interpretation problem is real and must be attended to by the experimentalists, but it cannot plausibly explain away the vast amounts of evidence for cognitive biases. The weakest of Cohen's claims, in our view, is the *external validity problem*: that psychological experiments are unrepresentative of the real world. They can be artificial, of course, but there are very many reported experiments that are carefully controlled pointing to clear evidence of cognitive biases. There have also been many demonstrations that biases demonstrated in the laboratory occur in real world contexts (see a number of the papers in the collection edited by Gilovich et al., 2002).

How far psychologists of reasoning should make normative evaluations of people's reasoning is a debatable question in psychological research, as we first discussed many years ago (Evans & Over, 1996). However, when Elqayam and Evans (2011) went so far as to propose a descriptivist approach in which we would essentially do away with normative evaluations in the psychology of reasoning, few of the commentators agreed with this, psychologists and philosophers alike. But since Cohen, psychologists have felt obliged to comment on rationality in a less simplistic manner. We explore some of the many ideas about rationality that have arisen in the remainder of this section.

7.2 Rationality and Dual Processing

Dual-process theory, the focus of Section 6, has been linked in various ways with human rationality. Consider the basic distinction between *epistemic* and *instrumental* rationality (Kolodny & Brunero, 2023). Organisms have instrumental rationality to the extent that they can reliably achieve their individual goals. Epistemic rationality is the acquisition and maintenance of well-supported beliefs. Epistemic rationality was long thought of as a human characteristic, but more recent studies of non-human animal cognition cast some doubts on this tradition. The notion that Type 2 or System 2 thinking is uniquely human, which has been suggested by various authors (e.g., Evans & Over, 1996; Reber, 1993; Stanovich, 2004) is not strictly correct as pointed out by the biologist Toates (2004, 2006). Higher animals have working memory and two different kinds of learning, one based on association and the other on encoding of individual, episodic events (Schacter, 1987). We think it more accurate to say that the second system (which does Type 2 processing) became uniquely *developed* in human beings, due the evolution of greatly enlarged frontal lobes, high working memory capacity, and capacities for language and suppositional reasoning (Evans, 2010).

We refer to this development as the *new mind*, which was added to the *old mind* which still shares many features with the minds of other animals, including basic emotions and associative learning systems. Humans consequently have a unique ability to reason about hypothetical possibilities. Stanovich (2011) has made a similar distinction between an autonomous and a reflective mind. Our instrumental rationality derives partially from associative learning systems in the old mind that we share with other animals, as well as innate cognitive modules underlying, for example, the visual system and language processing which operate entirely outside of consciousness. But it also depends on the epistemic rationality of the new mind with its highly developed capacity for acquiring, storing, retrieving, and reasoning about explicit knowledge and belief.

Evans (2013) has written about the differences in rationality of the two minds. Old mind rationality in humans and other animals is driven by the past. We evolved cognitive modules by adaptation to past environments, and we learn within our lifetimes to adapt our behaviour to the current environment. Much of this learning is Skinnerian: we repeat activities which have been reinforced in the past and avoid those which were punishing. This learning process can lead to helpful habits as well as destructive addictions, for example, pathological gambling, and phobias. New mind rationality is facilitated by hypothetical thinking or 'cognitive decoupling' (Evans & Stanovich, 2013) meaning that it can ignore the current context, and imagine scenarios not grounded in current beliefs about the actual state of the world. Such thinking can engage with both counterfactual possibilities and yet to be determined future possibilities. Hence we *can*, in the manner envisaged by decision theory, anticipate the future consequences of our actions and change our behaviour accordingly. But when the two minds are in conflict, the old often wins (Evans, 2010). For example, we go for short-term gratification and not the future benefit we prefer at a higher level. Yet, it is the new mind that makes us distinctively human and able to do many things unknown elsewhere in the animal kingdom, for example in the arts and sciences. To do these things we must maintain, at least to some extent, logically coherent belief systems and reason with them well enough for our purposes.

Keith Stanovich (e.g., Stanovich, 2004, 2011, 2018) has written extensively about rationality within a dual-process framework. His autonomous mind contains a mixture of innate cognitive modules, implicit knowledge acquired by associative learning, and knowledge which was once explicit and has become automated by practice. He has argued, intriguingly, that other animals are often *more* instrumentally rational than humans, at least as conventionally measured by normative decision theory (Stanovich, 2013). This is because animals always pursue immediate goals, while humans have layers of complexity of higher-order values and conflicting goals in their reflective minds. A good example of a human bias is *sunk costs*. Imagine you bought expensive opera tickets months ago but when the night comes you are exhausted, and your favourite football team is on TV. Right now, you would rather stay home and watch the game than go to the opera. In normative decision theory, that is what you should do because the cost of the tickets is sunk, the same whether you go out or stay in. But most people would nevertheless go to the opera because they would not like the thought of 'wasting' money, or perhaps because they like to think they are sophisticated people who prefer opera to football. Of course, we could argue that their choice is rational in a sense not captured by the instrumental rationality of pursuing immediate goals.

Stanovich has argued that normative problem-solving and decision-making depends on a number of factors. You must first recognise that the problem in front of you cannot be solved by habit or pattern recognition. Then you must apply the necessary cognitive effort, you must have sufficient cognitive capacity to solve the problem and you must have relevant *mindware*, or knowledge of how to solve it. Mindware is a key concept (Stanovich, 2018): rationality depends on education and training as well. Other authors have, by contrast, praised the role of intuition and 'gut feelings' in rational decision making (e.g., Gigerenzer, 2007; Gladwell, 2005). Both perspectives have their merits. Intuitions can save lives (see Klein, 1998, for examples) and pattern recognition, derived from experiential learning, has a key role in expert problem-solving. But Stanovich emphasises that in a modern technological world, reliance on intuitions can be dangerous and a rational thinking style highly advantageous. Our cognitive miserliness evolved in a very different world from that in which we live now.

7.3 Bayesian Reasoning and Instrumental Rationality

It is impossible to check our beliefs, above the level of very restricted and limited ones, for full logical coherence, as defined by normative Bayesianism.

It is computationally too difficult, and sometimes logically impossible, to ensure coherence and classical consistency in our beliefs in general. The singularity principle (Evans, 2007a), which posits that people tend to focus on one hypothesis at a time, can give them local coherence in immediate reasoning, allowing them to reach some goals and have instrumental rationality to this extent, despite incoherence or inconsistency with other beliefs they hold. It is equally true that full logical coherence is too weak as a condition to guarantee that we achieve our real-world goals. Some people with severe clinical delusions, for example, of a paranoid nature, could be coherent in their subjective delusional beliefs and yet be failing miserably to achieve their goals of having a happy and fulfilling life. Thus, full logical coherence is neither necessary nor sufficient for instrumental rationality.

There is much more, however, to Bayesianism than being coherent, and it is far more difficult to specify exactly how it as a whole is related to instrumental rationality. In Section 3.4, we saw that Bayesian conditionalisation is a normative proposal about how we should update or revise our beliefs. There are arguments and even proofs, under certain assumptions, that we will come to agree in our beliefs if we use strict Bayesian conditionalisation to update them. In 3.4 we used the example of trying to find out whether a certain coin was double-headed or fair. Some of us might start out by assigning an equal prior probability of .5 to these two possibilities, while other people judge that the coin is quite likely to be fair and assign a probability of .75 to that. But now if the coin is repeatedly spun and comes up heads again and again, and we all follow the procedure of strict conditionalisation, agreeing that invariance holds, and remaining coherent in our beliefs, then we will all get closer and closer to agreeing that the coin is double-headed. Our separate priors will be 'washed out', and there will be *convergence* in our beliefs. There are even arguments that such convergence is what is meant by scientific objectivity or truth (see Sprenger & Hartmann, 2019, and the references given there for these convergence arguments and proofs and critical evaluations of them).

Well-confirmed scientific hypotheses and theories, by Bayesian belief updating, can obviously be used to achieve many goals, some of which have the greatest importance for our survival as individuals and a species. Even so, not everyone has the goal of scientific truth in the first place. Scientists should have it but sometimes do not. Fanatics and propagandists can be indifferent or even hostile to it. Perhaps propagandists have to use some Bayesian belief updating to find the best ways of persuading people of some point of view. But fanatics could simply refuse to acknowledge the existence of scientific evidence. They might, for example, refuse to accept the word of scientific experts and appeal to their own 'experts', as defined by their myside bias.

Social media algorithms also have the effect of encouraging users to access only the opinions of others that accord with their own, with or without probative evidence.

Stanovich (2021) considers at length whether myside bias is really a bias at all and whether it should be considered to be irrational. As mentioned earlier (Section 6.2), what sets myside bias measures apart from all other cognitive biases is that they are *not* related to general intelligence or rational thinking measures. The extent of the 'bias' is actually predicted by something different: the strength of the core belief which is influencing the thinking. Referring to the Bayesian framework, Stanovich points out that the diagnosticity (Section 3.5) of the evidence should be assessed independently of prior belief, before the two are combined to conform to Bayes' theorem (Section 3.4). But whether or not Bayesian procedures are properly followed, prior beliefs can vary widely between people and have a major impact on their reasoning.

Many psychologists, for example, would reject apparently strong statistical evidence for extra-sensory perception due to a firm prior belief that ESP is intrinsically most unlikely. Myside bias is particularly evident for topics on which there is a deep binary division of opinion, such as the case for the UK leaving or remaining in the European Union in 2016. In such cases, Stanovich notes that each side often holds that the other must be less educated or intelligent, or gullible in accepting weak or unsubstantiated arguments. But the evidence can suggest that they are not: they may simply have differing beliefs and values. Myside bias is not about *factual* beliefs. Compare our personal beliefs that (a) the UK has left the EU and (b) that the UK should one day re-join the EU. Only the former is verifiable against objective evidence. There are no clear objective grounds for establishing the 'should' in (b).

Rationality can reside in the beliefs people hold rather than the reasoning they do. Consider again people with actual clinical delusions such as those who have paranoia (Rhodes et al., 2020). They may 'hear' voices, and their new mind, Type 2 processing may have the goal, which only a human being could have, of explaining these occurrences. The result could be the inference that they are being spied on, giving them the satisfaction of goal achievement and to that extent instrumental rationality. Experiments have found that people with delusions can tend to jump to conclusions given limited evidence (see Rhodes et al., 2020, for points about these results), but in some instances, the inference to the explanation of being spied on could satisfy Bayesian principles, with the problem simply being hallucinatory premises. As we have already noted, paranoid delusions may prevent some people from achieving many life goals, but that might not hold for other individuals if their paranoia is not very severe.

How far people with even clinical delusions fail to achieve instrumental rationality, caused by violating Bayesian or other normative principles, has to be investigated on an individual basis.

Some limited conformity to logical and Bayesian principles is a necessary condition for us to have hypothetical thoughts and Type 2 processing to begin with, before these are assessed for their contribution to instrumental rationality. As we reported in Section 3.2, people do have an above chance tendency to conform to p-validity and be coherent, and MP has an especially high endorsement rate. The existence of hypothetical thought most clearly depends on some correct use of MP in particular, even though that that might sometimes take place when there is not full logical coherence.

7.4 Conclusions

Psychologists and philosophers alike have been engaged in a debate about the implications for human rationality of experimental research on human reasoning and judgement and decision-making. The frequently reported conflicts between human responses and presupposed normative systems initially led to concerns that humans might be fundamentally irrational. However, the past fifty years or so that debate has become much more complex and nuanced, in part triggered by the contribution of philosophers (Cohen, 1981), but also by a growing conviction among psychologists that humans could not have achieved what they have if they were irrational. This has led to detailed scrutiny of presupposed normative systems, as evidenced by the new paradigm psychology of reasoning. It is now more common to consider Bayesian principles, rather than classical logic, as yardsticks for normative reasoning. But this general tendency leaves many questions open. Good (1983) characterised 46,656 different varieties of normative Bayesians. Elqayam and Evans (2013) distinguished between strict and (their preferred) soft Bayesian approaches in the scientific study of human reasoning, and there is not yet wide agreement in the psychology of reasoning on the best specific approach to take.

Whether our reasoning has instrumental rationality in any given case can sometimes be extremely difficult to determine, partly due to the complexity of the human brain/mind. In some respects, people act like other animals, learning by experience what is good and bad for them and achieving instrumental rationality in this way. But the evolved addition of the distinctively human 'new mind' adds layers of complexity in which people can have multiple goals, sometimes in conflict with one another and reflecting uniquely human value systems. That is why it can be so hard to decide if someone's myside thinking is a cognitive bias. A key aim in the new mind is the attempt to maintain at least a locally coherent belief system, and it appears that cannot be achieved without creating a cognitive frame which encourages myside thinking to some extent. On the other hand, it is clear that myside thinking can undermine instrumental rationality, for example, when people act on the advice of 'experts' defined by their myside thinking instead of experts more reliably identified (Section 4.2) or seek out only the views of those who already agree with them, a process facilitated in the modern age by social media.

8 Overall Conclusions

Psychologists have been studying human reasoning intensively since the 1960s with much use of the traditional deduction paradigm for the first thirty to forty years that period. This method instructed people to ignore prior beliefs and draw only conclusions that necessarily followed from assumed premises, and it used standard binary logic as a normative system for deciding accuracy. The review of hundreds of such studies in Evans et al. (1993) made it clear that humans are poor reasoners by those standards, even those of higher intelligence and education levels. First, they make many logical errors, especially by endorsing inferences with conclusions that do not necessarily follow given the premises. Second, they are systematically biased by irrelevant linguistic and structural features of the arguments presented. Finally, people have great difficulty in ignoring the prior beliefs that are stimulated by the content and context of the problems presented. The last finding is strikingly the case for the those of measured lower cognitive ability, even within university student populations.

These kinds of results caused a major debate about the rationality of human reasoning. Philosophers and psychologists were both engaged, and they presented a paradox to reasoning researchers. How could human have achieved their astonishing advances in science, engineering, and the arts, which so clearly set them apart from other animals, if they were fundamentally irrational? The conclusion eventually reached by most psychologists was that the problem lies in the presupposed normative system: binary logic is simply not a good yardstick for rational reasoning in the real world. Human reasoning is in fact inherently belief based and probabilistic. This conclusion led in turn to what is known as the new paradigm in the psychology of reasoning.

The new paradigm recognises that human reasoning usually consists of drawing probable conclusions from degrees of belief as premises, or from some contextually relevant hypothetical possibilities, and is often directed towards revising or updating degrees of belief. It aims to account for this reasoning using subjective probability theory and the Bayesian account of belief updating. It is supported by experimental results broadly confirming that people judge the probability of a natural language conditional, $P(if\ p\ then\ q)$, to be the conditional probability of q given p, $P(q|p)$. The introduction of Bayesian accounts of reasoning into the psychology of reasoning has yielded many new results in the field. There is some tendency for people to be coherent and to conform to probabilistic validity, p-validity, in their reasoning, especially when the inferences are explicitly presented as listed premises with a conclusion. But they are still not perfect, and sometimes their reasoning is fallacious, and their judgements biased.

The broader questions associated with human reasoning discussed over the past fifty years or so have concerned dual-process theory and rationality, each given a section at the end of this Element. Dual-process theory has ancient roots in philosophy and has also been manifested in many independent versions throughout cognitive and social psychology (Frankish & Evans, 2009). The version that developed within the psychology of reasoning started out largely as an attempt to explain the frequent observation of cognitive fallacies and biases, with the idea that unconscious Type 1 processes responsible for biases somehow compete with or pre-empt more rational Type 2 processes. The second author, who helped to develop these early accounts, came to realise later that there is a much broader family of such theories be found in diverse fields, including the studies of cognitive social psychology, implicit learning, decision making, attention and working memory and other fields. A possible explanation of many findings is the evolution of a new mind, distinctively developed in human beings for Type 2 processing, which is added to and may compete with an older mind similar to that found in other higher animals.

At the end of this Element, we focused on rationality and studies of human reasoning, a topic which fascinates philosophers and psychologists alike. It has been debated extensively since the 1980s. The first major challenge came from Cohen (1981), who pointed out, as a philosopher, that psychologists were relying on classical logic and not considering other logics. He also questioned the validity of laboratory experiments on several grounds. His arguments certainly helped stimulate the dissatisfaction with the traditional methods which later resulted in the new paradigm. The development of dual-process and two-minds theories also complicated the debate about rationality, which is really much more complex than the search for the right normative system. The human mind is multi-layered, with both specialised and general inferential systems, and is capable of having many goals and values which may conflict with one another. It needs to strive for coherence to avoid chaos, and in the process manifests myside thinking. All of these factors can compromise instrumental rationality, defined as the successful pursuit of goals. But for all its flaws, the ability of the human mind to reason effectively in many domains is an extraordinary achievement.

References

Adams, E. (1965). The logic of conditionals. *Inquiry*, *8*, 166–197.

Adams, E. (1998). *A primer of probability logic*. Stanford: CLSI.

Baddeley, A. (2007). *Working memory, thought and action*. Oxford: Oxford University Press.

Baddeley, A. (2020). *Exploring working memory: Selected works of Alan Baddelely*. London: Routledge.

Baratgin, J., Over, D. E., & Politzer, G. (2013). Uncertainty and the de Finetti tables. *Thinking & Reasoning*, *19*, 308–328.

Baratgin, J., Politzer, G., Over, D. E., & Takahashi, T. (2018). The psychology of uncertainty and three-valued truth tables. *Frontiers in Psychology*, *9*, 1479.

Barbey, A. K., & Sloman, S. A. (2007). Base-rate respect: From ecological rationality to dual processes. *Behavioral and Brain Sciences*, *30*, 241–297.

Boissin, E., Josserand, M., De Neys, W., & Caparos, S. (2024). Debiasing thinking among non-WEIRD reasoners. *Cognition*, *243*(3), 105681.

Bonnefon, J.-F. (2013). New ambitions for a new paradigm: Putting the psychology of reasoning at the service of humanity. *Thinking & Reasoning*, *19*(3–4), 381–398.

Bourlier, M., Jacquet, J., Lassiter, D., & Baratgin, J. (2023). Coherence, not conditional meaning, accounts for the relevance effect. *Frontiers in Psychology*, *14*, 1150550.

Braine, M. D. S., & O'Brien, D. P. (1991). A theory of if: A lexical entry, reasoning program, and pragmatic principles. *Psychological Review*, *98*, 182–203.

Byrne, R. M. J. (1989). Suppressing valid inferences with conditionals. *Cognition*, *31*, 61–83.

Cantwell, J. (2020). Revisiting McGee's probabilistic analysis of conditionals. *Journal of Philosophical logic*, *5*, 1–45.

Chater, N., & Oaksford, M. (1999). The probability heuristics model of syllogistic reasoning. *Cognitive Psychology*, *38*, 191–258.

Cleeremans, A. (2015). *Implicit learning and consciousness*. London: Routledge.

Cleeremans, A., & Kuvaldina, M. (2019). *Implicit learning: 50 years on*. London: Routledge.

Cohen, L. J. (1981). Can human irrationality be experimentally demonstrated? *Behavioral and Brain Sciences*, *4*, 317–370.

Cosmides, L., & Tooby, J. (1996). Are humans good intuitive statisticians after all? Rethinking some conclusions from the literature on judgment under uncertainty. *Cognition*, *58*, 1–73.

Corbett, B., Feeney, A., & McCormack, T. (2023). Prosocial risk taking and interpersonal regret in children: An individual differences study. *Social Development, 32,* 171–187.

Cruz, N. (2020). Deduction from uncertain premises? In S. Elqayam, I. Douven, J. St. B. T. Evans, & N. Cruz (Eds.), *Logic and uncertainty in the human mind* (pp. 27–41). Abingdon: Routledge.

Cruz, N., Baratgin, J., Oaksford, M., & Over, D. E. (2015). Bayesian reasoning with ifs and ands and ors. *Frontiers in Psychology, 6,* 192.

Cruz, N., & Over, D. E. (2023). Independence conditionals. In S. Kaufmann, D. E. Over, & G. Sharma (Eds.), *Conditionals – Logic, linguistics and psychology* (pp. 223–233). London: Palgrave Macmillan.

Cruz, N., & Over, D. E. (2024). From de Finetti's three values to conditional probabilities in the psychology of reasoning. In P. Egré, & L. Rossi (Eds.), *Handbook of trivalent logics*. Cambridge, MA: MIT Press.

Cruz, N., Over, D., Oaksford, M., & Baratgin, J. (2016). Centering and the meaning of conditionals. In A. Papafragou, D. Grodner, D. Mirman, & J. C. Trueswell (Eds.), *Proceedings of the 38th annual conference of the cognitive science society* (pp. 1104–1109). Austin, TX: Cognitive Science Society.

Cruz, N., Over, D., & Oaksford, M. (2017). The elusive oddness of or-introduction. In G. Gunzelmann, A. Howes, T. Tenbrink, & E. Davelaar (Eds.), *The 39th annual meeting of the cognitive science society* (pp. 663–668). London: Cognitive Science Society.

De Finetti, B. (1936/1995). The logic of probability. *Philosophical Studies, 77,* 181–190.

De Finetti, B. (1937/1964). Foresight: Its logical laws, its subjective sources. In H. E. Kyburg, & H. E. Smokier (Eds.), *Studies in subjective probability* (pp. 55–118). New York: Wiley.

De Neys, W. (2012). Bias and conflict: A case for logical intuitions. *Perspectives on Psychological Science, 7,* 28–38.

De Neys, W. (2022). Advancing theorizing about fast-and-slow thinking. *Behavioral and Brain Sciences, 46,* e111.

Doherty, M. E., Mynatt, C. R., Tweney, R. D., & Schiavo, M. D. (1979). Pseudodiagnosticity. *Acta Psychologica, 43,* 11–21.

Douven, I., Elqayam, S., & Krzyżanowska, K. (2023). Inferentialism: A manifesto. In S. Kaufmann, D. E. Over, & G. Sharma (Eds.), *Conditionals – Logic, linguistics and psychology* (pp. 175–221). London: Palgrave Macmillan.

Deary, I. J. (2020). *Intelligence: A very short introduction.* Oxford: Oxford University Press.

Demey, L., Kooi, B., & Sack, J. (2023). Logic and probability. *The Stanford Encyclopedia of Philosophy*. E. N. Zalta, & U. Nodelman (Eds.), https://plato.stanford.edu/archives/fall2023/entries/logic-probability/.

Edgington, D. (1995). On conditionals. *Mind*, *104*, 235–329.

Egré, P., Rossi, L., & Sprenger, J. (2021). De Finettian logics of indicative conditionals. *Journal of Philosophical Logic*, *50*, 187–213.

Elqayam, S., & Evans, J. St. B. T. (2011). Subtracting 'ought' from 'is': Descriptivism versus normativism in the study of human thinking. *Behavioral and Brain Sciences*, *34*, 233–290.

Elqayam, S., & Evans, J. St. B. T. (2013). Rationality in the new paradigm: Strict versus soft Bayesian approaches. *Thinking & Reasoning*, *19*, 453–470.

Engle, R. W. (2002). Working memory capacity as executive attention. *Current Directions in Psychological Science*, *11*, 19–23.

Epstein, S. (1994). Integration of the cognitive and psychodynamic unconscious. *American Psychologist*, *49*, 709–724.

Evans, J. St. B. T. (1989). *Bias in human reasoning: Causes and consequences*. Brighton: Erlbaum.

Evans, J. St. B. T. (2002). Logic and human reasoning: An assessment of the deduction paradigm. *Psychological Bulletin*, *128*, 978–996.

Evans, J. St. B. T. (2005). *How to do research: A psychologist's guide*. Hove: Psychology Press.

Evans, J. St. B. T. (2006). The heuristic-analytic theory of reasoning: Extension and evaluation. *Psychonomic Bulletin & Review*, *13*, 378–395.

Evans, J. St. B. T. (2007a). *Hypothetical thinking: Dual processes in reasoning and judgement*. Hove: Psychology Press.

Evans, J. St. B. T. (2007b). On the resolution of conflict in dual-process theories of reasoning. *Thinking & Reasoning*, *13*, 321–329.

Evans, J. St. B. T. (2010). *Thinking twice: Two minds in one brain*. Oxford: Oxford University Press.

Evans, J. St. B. T. (2014). Two minds rationality. *Thinking & Reasoning*, *20*, 129–146.

Evans, J. St. B. T. (2016). Reasoning, biases and dual processes: The lasting impact of Wason (1960). *The Quarterly Journal of Experimental Psychology*, *69*(10), 1–17.

Evans, J. St. B. T. (2018). Dual-process theory: Perspectives and problems. In W. De Neys (Ed.), *Dual process theory 2.0* (pp. 137–155). London: Routledge.

Evans, J. St. B. T. (2019). Reflections on reflection: The nature and function of type 2 processes in dual-process theories of reasoning. *Thinking & Reasoning*, *25*(4), 383–415.

Evans, J. St. B. T. (2021). The rationality debate in the psychology of reasoning: A historical review. In M. Knauff, & W. Spohn (Eds.), *The handbook of rationality* (pp. 71–86). Cambridge, MA: MIT Press.

Evans, J. St. B. T. (2022). Wason selection task. In R. F. Pohl (Ed.), *Cognitive illusions: Intriguing phenomena in thinking, judgment and memory* (pp. 140–153). New York: Routledge.

Evans, J. St. B. T. (2020). The suppositional conditional is not (just) the probability conditional. In S. Elqayam, I. Douven, J. St. B. T. Evans, & N. Cruz (Eds.), *Logic and uncertainty in the human mind* (pp. 57–70). Abingdon: Routledge.

Evans, J. St. B. T., Ball, L. J., & Thompson, V. A. (2022). Belief bias in deductive reasoning. In R. F. Pohl (Ed.), *Cognitive illusions: Intriguing phenomena in thinking, judgement and memory* (pp. 154–172). New York: Routledge.

Evans, J. St. B. T., Barston, J. L., & Pollard, P. (1983). On the conflict between logic and belief in syllogistic reasoning. *Memory & Cognition, 11*, 295–306.

Evans, J. St. B. T., & Curtis-Holmes, J. (2005). Rapid responding increases belief bias: Evidence for the dual-process theory of reasoning. *Thinking & Reasoning, 11*(4), 382–389.

Evans, J. St. B. T., Handley, S., Neilens, H., & Over, D. E. (2007). Thinking about conditionals: A study of individual differences. *Memory & Cognition, 35*, 1772–1784.

Evans, J. St. B. T., Handley, S., Neilens, H., & Over, D. E. (2010). The influence of cognitive ability and instructional set on causal conditional inference. *Quarterly Journal of Experimental Psychology, 63*(5), 892–909.

Evans, J. St. B. T., Handley, S. J., Harper, C., & Johnson-Laird, P. N. (1999). Reasoning about necessity and possibility: A test of the mental model theory of deduction. *Journal of Experimental Psychology: Learning Memory and Cognition, 25*, 1495–1513.

Evans, J. St. B. T., Handley, S. J., & Over, D. E. (2003). Conditionals and conditional probability. *Journal of Experimental Psychology: Learning Memory and Cognition, 29*, 321–335.

Evans, J. St. B. T., & Lynch, J. S. (1973). Matching bias in the selection task. *British Journal of Psychology, 64*, 391–397.

Evans, J. St. B. T., Newstead, S. E., & Byrne, R. M. J. (1993). *Human reasoning: The psychology of deduction*. Hove: Erlbaum.

Evans, J. St. B. T., & Over, D. E. (1996). *Rationality and reasoning*. Hove: Psychology Press.

Evans, J. St. B. T., & Over, D. E. (2004). *If*. Oxford: Oxford University Press.

Evans, J. St. B. T. (2013). Two minds rationality. *Thinking & Reasoning, 20*, 129–146.

Evans, J. St. B. T., & Stanovich, K. E. (2013). Dual process theories of higher cognition: Advancing the debate. *Perspectives on Psychological Science, 8*, 223–241.

Evans, J. St. B. T., Thompson, V., & Over, D. E. (2015). Uncertain deduction and conditional reasoning. *Frontiers in Psychology, 6*, 398.

Evans, J. St. B. T., & Wason, P. C. (1976). Rationalisation in a reasoning task. *British Journal of Psychology, 63*, 205–212.

Frankish, K., & Evans, J. St. B. T. (2009). The duality of mind: An historical perspective. In J. St. B. T. Evans, & K. Frankish (Eds.), *In two minds: Dual processes and beyond* (pp. 1–30). Oxford: Oxford University Press.

Frederick, S. (2005). Cognitive reflection and decision making. *Journal of Economic Perspectives, 19*(4), 25–42.

Feeney, A. (2018). Forty years of progress on category-based inductive reasoning. In L. J. Ball, & V. A. Thompson (Eds.), *International handbook of thinking and reasoning* (pp. 167–185). Hove: Psychology Press.

Ghasemi, O., Handley, S. J., Howarth, S., Newman, I. R., & Thompson, V. A. (2022). Logical intuition is not really about logic. *Journal of Experimental Psychology: General, 151*, 2009–2028.

Ghasemi, O., Handley, S. J., Howarth, S. (2023). Illusory intuitive inferences: Matching heuristics explain logical intuitions. *Cognition, 235*, 105417.

Gigerenzer, G. (2007). *Gut feelings: The intelligence of the unconscious.* London: Penguin.

Gigerenzer, G., & Hoffrage, U. (1995). How to improve Bayesian reasoning without instruction: Frequency formats. *Psychological Review, 102*, 684–704.

Gilio, A., & Over, D. E. (2012). The psychology of inferring conditionals from disjunctions: A probabilistic study. *Journal of Mathematical Psychology, 56*, 118–131.

Gilio, A., Pfeifer, N., & Sanfilippo, G. (2020). Probabilistic entailment and iterated conditionals. In S. Elqayam, I. Douven, J. St. B. T. Evans, & N. Cruz (Eds.), *Logic and uncertainty in the human mind* (pp. 71–101). Abingdon: Routledge.

Gilovich, T., Griffin, D., & Kahneman, D. (2002). *Heuristics and biases: The psychology of intuitive judgement.* Cambridge: Cambridge University Press.

Gladwell, M. (2005). *Blink.* London: Penguin.

Good, I. J. (1983). *Good thinking: The foundations of probability and its applications.* Minneapolis: University of Minnesota Press.

Goodwin, R. Q., & Wason, P. C. (1972). Degrees of insight. *British Journal of Psychology, 63*, 205–212.

Grice, P. (1989). *Studies in the way of words.* Cambridge, MA: Harvard University Press.

Hadjichristidis, C., Sloman, S. A., & Over, D. E. (2014). Categorical induction from uncertain premises: Jeffrey's doesn't completely rule. *Thinking & Reasoning, 20*, 405–431.

Hahn, U., & Oaksford, M. (2007). The rationality of informal argumentation: A Bayesian approach to reasoning fallacies. *Psychological Review, 114*, 704–732.

Handley, S. J., Newstead, S. E., & Trippas, D. (2011). Logic, beliefs, and instruction: A test of the default interventionist account of belief bias. *Journal of Experimental Psychology-Learning Memory and Cognition, 37*(1), 28–43.

Harris, A., J. L., Hahn, U., Madsen, J. K., & Hsu, A. S. (2016). The appeal to expert opinion: Quantitative support for a Bayesian network approach. *Cognitive Science, 40*, 1496–1533.

Henle, M. (1962). On the relation between logic and thinking. *Psychological Review, 69*, 366–378.

Howson, C., & Urbach, P. (2006). *Scientific reasoning: The Bayesian approach* (third edition). Chicago, IL: Open Court.

Inhelder, B., & Piaget, J. (1958). *The growth of logical thinking*. New York: Basic Books.

Jeffrey, R. C. (1983). *The logic of decision* (second edition). Chicago, IL: University of Chicago Press.

Jeffrey, R. C. (1991). Matter of fact conditionals. *Aristotelian Society Supplementary Volume, 65*, 161–183.

Johnson-Laird, P. N. (1983). *Mental models*. Cambridge: Cambridge University Press.

Johnson-Laird, P. N., & Bara, B. G. (1984). Syllogistic inference. *Cognition, 16*, 1–61.

Johnson-Laird, P. N., & Byrne, R. M. J. (1991). *Deduction*. Hove: Erlbaum.

Johnson-Laird, P. N., Khemlani, S., & Goodwin, G. P. (2015). Logic, probability, and human reasoning. *Trends in Cognitive Science, 19*, 201–214.

Kahneman, D. (2011). *Thinking, fast and slow*. New York: Farrar, Straus and Giroux.

Kahneman, D., Slovic, P., & Tversky, A. (1982). *Judgment under uncertainty: Heuristics and biases*. Cambridge: Cambridge University Press.

Kaufmann, S. (2023). How fake is fake past? In S. Kaufmann, D. E. Over, & G. Sharma (Eds.), *Conditionals – Logic, linguistics and psychology* (pp. 389–423). London: Palgrave Macmillan.

Keren, G., & Schul, Y. (2009). Two is not always better than one: A critical evaluation of two-system theories. *Perspectives on Psychological Science, 4*, 533–550.

Klayman, J., & Ha, Y. W. (1987). Confirmation, disconfirmation and information in hypothesis testing. *Psychological Review, 94*, 211–228

Klein, G. (1998). *Sources of power*. Cambridge, MA: MIT Press.

Kleiter, G. D. (1994). Natural sampling: Rationality without base rates. In G. H. Fisher, & D. Laming (Eds.), *Contributions to mathematical psychology, psychometrics, and methodology* (pp. 375–388). New York: Springer.

Kleiter, G. D., Fugard, J. B., Pfeifer, N. (2018). A process model of the understanding of uncertain conditionals. *Thinking & Reasoning, 24*, 386–422.

Kneale, W., & Kneale, M. (1962). *The development of logic*. Oxford: Oxford University Press.

Kolodny, N., & Brunero, J. (2023). Instrumental rationality. *The Stanford Encyclopedia of Philosophy*. E. N. Zalta, & U. Nodelman (Eds.), https://plato.stanford.edu/archives/sum2023/entries/rationality-instrumental/.

Kruglanski, A. W., & Gigerenzer, G. (2011). Intuitive and deliberative judgements are based on common principles. *Psychological Review, 118*(1), 97–109.

Lassiter, D. (2019). What we can learn from how trivalent conditionals avoid triviality. *Inquiry, 63*, 1087–1114.

Lassiter, D. (2023). Decomposing relevance in conditionals. *Mind & Language, 38*(3), 644–668.

Lassiter, D., & Goodman, N. D. (2015). How many kinds of reasoning? Inference, probability, and natural language semantics. *Cognition, 136*, 123–134.

Lewis, D. (1973). *Counterfactuals*. Cambridge, MA: Harvard University Press.

Lewis, D. (1976). Probabilities of conditionals and conditional probabilities. *Philosophical Review, 85*, 297–315.

Lucas, E. J., & Ball, L. J. (2005). Think-aloud protocols and the selection task: Evidence for relevance effects and rationalisation processes. *Thinking and Reasoning, 11*(1), 35–66.

Manktelow, K. I. (2021). *Beyond reasoning: The life, time and work of Peter Wason, pioneering psychologist*. Abingdon: Routledge.

McDowell, M., & Jacobs, P. (2017). Meta-analysis of the effect of natural frequencies on Bayesian reasoning. *Psychological Bulletin, 143*, 1273–1312.

Mercier, H., & Sperber, D. (2011). Why do humans reason? Arguments for an argumentative theory. *Behavioral and Brain Sciences, 34*, 57–111.

Mercier, H., & Sperber, D. (2017). *The enigma of reason: A new theory of human understanding*. Cambridge, MA: Harvard University Press.

Morley, N. J., Evans, J. St. B. T., & Handley, S. J. (2004). Belief bias and figural bias in syllogistic reasoning. *Quarterly Journal of Experimental Psychology, 57*(4), 666–692.

Newstead, S. E., Handley, S. J., Harley, C., Wright, H., & Farelly, D. (2004). Individual differences in deductive reasoning. *Quarterly Journal of Experimental Psychology, 57A*, 33–60.

Oakhill, J., Johnson-Laird, P. N., & Garnham, A. (1989). Believability and syllogistic reasoning. *Cognition, 31*, 117–140.

Oaksford, M., & Chater, N. (1994). A rational analysis of the selection task as optimal data selection. *Psychological Review, 101*, 608–631.

Oaksford, M., & Chater, N. (2007). *Bayesian rationality: The probabilistic approach to human reasoning*. Oxford: Oxford University Press.

Oaksford, M., & Chater, N. (2020). New paradigms in the psychology of reasoning. *Annual Review of Psychology, 71*, 305–330.

Oberauer, K., & Wilhelm, O. (2003). The meaning(s) of conditionals: Conditional probabilities, mental models and personal utilities. *Journal of Experimental Psychology: Learning Memory and Cognition, 29*, 680–693.

Oberauer, K., Weidenfeld, A., & Fischer, K. (2007). What makes us believe a conditional? *Thinking & Reasoning, 13*(4), 340–369.

Osman, M. (2004). An evaluation of dual-process theories of reasoning. *Psychonomic Bulletin and Review, 11*(6), 988–1010.

Over, D. E. (2003). From massive modularity to metarepresentation: The evolution of higher cognition. In D. E. Over (Ed.), *Evolution and the psychology of thinking: The debate* (pp. 121–144). Hove: The Psychology Press.

Over, D. E. (2009). New paradigm psychology of reasoning. *Thinking & Reasoning, 15*, 431–438.

Over, D. E. (2020). The development of the new paradigm in the psychology of reasoning. In S. Elqayam, I. Douven, J. St. B. T. Evans, & N. Cruz (Eds.), *Logic and uncertainty in the human mind* (pp. 431–438). Abingdon: Routledge.

Over, D. E. (2023a). The new paradigm and massive modalization: Commentary on Knauff and Gazzo Castañeda. *Thinking & Reasoning, 29*(3), 389–395.

Over, D. E. (2023b). Independence and rationality. *The Reasoner*: Focus issue on the *Handbook of Rationality, 17*(6), 47–48. www.thereasoner.org/.

Over, D. E., & Baratgin, J. (2017). The 'defective' truth table: Its past, present, and future. In N. Galbraith, D. E. Over, & E. Lucas, (Eds.), *The thinking mind: A Festschrift for Ken Manktelow* (pp. 15–28). Hove: Psychology Press.

Over, D. E., & Cruz, N. (2018). Probabilistic accounts of conditional reasoning. In L. J. Ball, & V. A. Thompson (Eds.), *International handbook of thinking and reasoning* (pp. 434–450). Hove: Psychology Press.

Over, D. E., & Cruz, N. (2023). Indicative and counterfactual conditionals in the psychology of reasoning. In S. Kaufmann, D. E. Over, & G. Sharma (Eds.),

Conditionals – Logic, linguistics and psychology (pp. 139–174). London: Palgrave Macmillan.

Over, D. E., Hadjichristidis, C., Evans, J. St. B. T., Handley, S. J., & Sloman, S. A. (2007). The probability of causal conditionals. *Cognitive Psychology, 54*, 62–97.

Pearl, J. (2000). *Causality: Models, reasoning, and inference.* Cambridge: Cambridge University Press.

Pearl, J. (2013). Structural counterfactuals: A brief introduction. *Cognitive Science, 37*, 977–985.

Pfeifer, N. (2023). The logic and pragmatics of conditionals under uncertainty: A mental probability logic perspective. In S. Kaufmann, D. E. Over, & G. Sharma (Eds.), *Conditionals – Logic, linguistics and psychology* (pp. 73–102). London: Palgrave Macmillan.

Pfeifer, N., & Kleiter, G. D. (2009). Framing human inference by coherence based probability logic. *Journal of Applied Logic, 7*, 206–217.

Poletiek, F. (2001). *Hypothesis-testing behaviour.* Hove: Psychology Press.

Politzer, G., Over, D. E., & Baratgin, J. (2010). Betting on conditionals. *Thinking & Reasoning, 16*, 172–197.

Popper, K. R. (1959). *The logic of scientific discovery.* London: Hutchinson.

Ramsey, F. P. (1926/1990). Truth and probability. In D. H. Mellor (Ed.), *Philosophical papers* (pp. 52–94). Cambridge: Cambridge University Press.

Ramsey, F. P. (1929/1990). General propositions and causality. In D. H. Mellor (Ed.), *Philosophical papers* (pp. 145–163). Cambridge: Cambridge University Press.

Reber, A. S. (1993). *Implicit learning and tacit knowledge.* Oxford: Oxford University Press.

Rhodes, S., Galbraith, N., & Manktelow, K. (2020). Delusional rationality. In S. Elqayam, I. Douven, J. St. B. T. Evans, & N. Cruz (Eds.), *Logic and uncertainty in the human mind* (pp. 178–191). Abingdon: Routledge.

Rips, L. J. (1994). *The psychology of proof.* Cambridge, MA: MIT Press.

Rothschild, D. (2023). Living in a material world: A critical notice of Suppose and tell. *Mind, 132*, 208–233.

Sanfilippo, G., Gilio, A., Over, D. E., & Pfeifer, N. (2020). Probabilities of conditionals and previsions of iterated conditionals. *International Journal of Approximate Reasoning, 121*, 150–173.

Schacter, D. L. (1987). Implicit memory: History and current status. *Journal of Experimental Psychology: Learning Memory and Cognition, 13*, 501–518.

Sebben, S., & Ullrich, J. (2021). Can conditionals explain explanations? A modus ponens model of B because A. *Cognition, 215*, 104812.

Shapiro, S., & Kouri Kissel, T. (2022). Classical logic. *The Stanford Encyclopedia of Philosophy*, E. N. Zalta & U. Nodelman (Eds.), https://plato.stanford.edu/archives/win2022/entries/logic-classical/.

Singmann, H., Klauer, K. C., & Over, D. E. (2014). New normative standards of conditional reasoning and the dual-source model. *Frontiers of Psychology*, *5*, 316.

Skovgaard-Olsen, N., Kellen, D., Krahl, H., & Klauer, K. C. (2017). Relevance differently affects the truth, acceptability, and probability evaluations of 'and', 'but', 'therefore', and 'if then'. *Thinking & Reasoning*, *23*, 449–482.

Skovgaard-Olsen, N., Singmann, H., & Klauer, K. C. (2016). The relevance effect and conditionals. *Cognition*, *150*, 26–36.

Sloman, S. A. (1996). The empirical case for two systems of reasoning. *Psychological Bulletin*, *119*, 3–22.

Sloman, S. A., & Fernbach, P. (2017). *The knowledge illusion: Why we never think alone*. New York: Riverhead.

Sloman, S. A., & Lagnado, D. A. (2015). Causality in thought. *Annual Review of Psychology*, *66*, 223–247.

Smedslund, J. (1970). Circular relation between understanding and logic. *Scandinavian Journal of Psychology*, *11*, 217–219.

Smith, E., & DeCoster, J. (1999). Associative and rule-based processing: A connectionist interpretation of dual-process models. In S. Chaiken, & Y. Trope (Eds.), *Dual-process theories in social psychology* (pp. 323–360). New York: The Guildford Press.

Spearman, C. (1904). General intelligence, objectively determined and measured. *American Journal of Psychology*, *15*, 201–293.

Sprenger, J., & Hartmann, S. (2019). *Bayesian philosophy of science*. Oxford: Oxford University Press.

Stalnaker, R. (1968). A theory of conditionals. In N. Rescher (Ed.), *Studies in logical theory* (pp. 98–112). Oxford: Blackwell.

Stanovich, K. E. (1999). *Who is rational? Studies of individual differences in reasoning*. Mahway, NJ: Lawrence Elrbaum Associates.

Stanovich, K. E. (2004). *The robot's rebellion: Finding meaning the age of Darwin*. Chicago, IL: University of Chicago Press.

Stanovich, K. E. (2009). *What intelligence tests miss*. London: Yale university press.

Stanovich, K. E. (2011). *Rationality and the reflective mind*. New York: Oxford University Press.

Stanovich, K. E. (2013). Why humans are (sometimes) less rational than other animals: Cognitive complexity and the axioms of rational choice. *Thinking & Reasoning*, *19*, 1–26.

Stanovich, K. E. (2018). Miserliness in human cognition: The interaction of detection, override and mindware. *Thinking & Reasoning, 24*, 423–444.

Stanovich, K. E. (2021). *The bias that divides us: The science and politics of myside thinking.* Cambridge, MA: MIT Press.

Stanovich, K. E., Sÿ, W. C., & West, R. F. (1999). The domain specificity and generality of belief bias: Searching for a generalizable critical thinking skill. *Journal of Educational Psychology, 91*(3), 497–510.

Stanovich, K. E., West, C., & Toplak, M. E. (2016). *The rationality quotient: Towards a test of ratiional thinking.* Cambridge, MA: MIT Press.

Stanovich, K. E., & West, R. F. (1998). Cognitive ability and variation in selection task performance. *Thinking & Reasoning, 4*, 193–230.

Stanovich, K. E., & West, R. F. (2000). Advancing the rationality debate. *Behavioral and Brain Sciences, 23*(5), 701–726.

Stevenson, R. J., & Over, D. E. (1995). Deduction from uncertain premises. *Quarterly Journal of Experimental Psychology, 48A*, 613–643.

Thompson, V. A. (1994). Interpretational factors in conditional reasoning. *Memory & Cognition, 22*, 742–758.

Thompson, V. A., & Byrne, R. M. J. (2002). Reasoning counterfactually: Making inferences about things that didn't happen. *Journal of Experimental Psychology: Learning, Memory, and Cognition, 28*, 1154–1170.

Thompson, V. A., Evans, J. St. B., & Campbell, J. I. D. (2013). Matching bias on the selection task: It's fast and feels good. *Thinking & Reasoning, 19*(3–4), 431–452.

Thompson, V. A., Pennycook, G., Trippas, D., & Evans, J. St. B. T. (2018). Do smart people have better intuitions? *Journal of Experimental Psychology: General, 147*, 945–961.

Thompson, V. A., Prowse Turner, J. A., & Pennycook, G. (2011). Intuition, reason, and metacognition. *Cognitive Psychology, 63*(3), 107–140.

Toates, F. (2004). In two minds – Consideration of evolutionary precursors permits a more integrative theory. *Trends in Cognitive Sciences, 8*(2), 57.

Toates, F. (2006). A model of the hierarchy of behaviour, cognition and consciousness. *Consciousness and Cognition, 15*, 75–118.

Toplak, M. E., West, R. F., & Stanovich, K. E. (2011). The cognitive reflection test as a predictor of performance on heuristics-and-biases tasks. *Memory & Cognition, 39*(7), 1275–1289.

Tversky, A., & Kahneman, D. (1974). Judgement under uncertainty: Heuristics and biases. *Science, 185*, 1124–1131.

Tversky, A., & Kahneman, D. (1983). Extensional vs intuitive reasoning: The conjunction fallacy in probability judgment. *Psychological Review, 90*, 293–315.

van Rooij, R., Krzyżanowska, K., & Douven, I. (2023). Williamson's abductive case for the material conditional account. *Studia Logica*, *111*, 653–685.

Wang, M., Over, D. E., & Liang, L. (2022). What is required for the truth of a general conditional? *Quarterly Journal of Experimental Psychology*, *75*, 11.

Wason, P. C. (1960). On the failure to eliminate hypotheses in a conceptual task. *Quarterly Journal of Experimental Psychology*, *12*, 12–40.

Wason, P. C. (1966). Reasoning. In B. M. Foss (Ed.), *New horizons in psychology I* (pp. 106–137). Harmandsworth: Penguin.

Wason, P. C. (1983). Realism and rationality in the selection task. In J. St. B. T. Evans (Ed.), *Thinking and reasoning: Psychological approaches* (pp. 44–75). London: Routledge & Kegan Paul.

Wason, P. C., & Evans, J. St. B. T. (1975). Dual processes in reasoning? *Cognition*, *3*, 141–154.

Wason, P. C., & Johnson-Laird, P. N. (1972). *Psychology of reasoning: Structure and content*. London: Batsford.

Wilkins, M. C. (1928). The effect of changed material on the ability to do formal syllogistic reasoning. *Archives of Psychology*, *16*, 102.

Williamson, T. (2020). *Suppose and tell: The semantics and heuristics of conditionals*. Oxford: Oxford University Press.

Woodworth, R. S., & Sells, S. B. (1935). An atmosphere effect in syllogistic reasoning. *Journal of Experimental Psychology*, *18*, 451–460.

Zhao, J., & Osherson, D. (2010). Updating beliefs in light of uncertain evidence: Descriptive assessment of Jeffrey's rule. *Thinking & Reasoning*, *16*(4), 288–307.

Zimmer, K. (2021). People may have used fire to clear forests more than 80,000 years ago. *Scientific American*. www.scientificamerican.com/article/people-may-have-used-fire-to-clear-forests-more-than-80-000-years-ago/.

Cambridge Elements ≡

Philosophy of Mind

Keith Frankish

The University of Sheffield

Keith Frankish is a philosopher specializing in philosophy of mind, philosophy of psychology, and philosophy of cognitive science. He is the author of *Mind and Supermind* (Cambridge University Press, 2004) and *Consciousness* (2005), and has also edited or coedited several collections of essays, including *The Cambridge Handbook of Cognitive Science* (Cambridge University Press, 2012), *The Cambridge Handbook of Artificial Intelligence* (Cambridge University Press, 2014) (both with William Ramsey), and *Illusionism as a Theory of Consciousness* (2017).

About the Series

This series provides concise, authoritative introductions to contemporary work in philosophy of mind, written by leading researchers and including both established and emerging topics. It provides an entry point to the primary literature and will be the standard resource for researchers, students, and anyone wanting a firm grounding in this fascinating field.

Cambridge Elements ☰

Philosophy of Mind

Elements in the Series

Imagination and Creative Thinking
Amy Kind

Attention and Mental Control
Carolyn Dicey Jennings

Biological Cognition
Bryce Huebner and Jay Schulkin

Embodied and Enactive Approaches to Cognition
Shaun Gallagher

Mental Content
Peter Schulte

Affective Bodily Awareness
Frédérique de Vignemont

The Computational Theory of Mind
Matteo Colombo and Gualtiero Piccinini

Memory and Remembering
Felipe De Brigard

Non-physicalist Theories of Consciousness
Hedda Hassel Mørch

Neurolaw
Gregg D. Caruso

Animal Minds
Marta Halina

Human Reasoning
David E. Over and Jonathan St B. T. Evans

A full series listing is available at: www.cambridge.org/EPMI

Printed in the United States
by Baker & Taylor Publisher Services